What the experts say about *Hou*

"This book is a winner! . . . . What makes this resource particularly effective is the fact that the author has conducted thousands of interviews, made hundreds of offers, and does indeed know what recruiters think."

—*Sandra L. McGuigan*
Director, Career Planning and Placement
Valparaiso University

"Here is advice from the person who hires! Job seekers will benefit from the straightforward, motivating, and entertaining insights offered by John LaFevre . . ."

—*Deborah Orr May*
Director, Career Planning and Placement
The University of Michigan

"An excellent book for *all* college students who one day will have to find a job."

—*Peter E. Veruki*
Director of Placement
School of Engineering & Applied Science
University of Virginia

"I know many people who could have made excellent use of this book after spending a lengthy time in the military service . . . Recommended reading for any job seeker."

—*Frank W. Elliot, Jr.*
Maj. General, U.S.A.F. (Ret.)

"This book will be a valuable tool for job seekers as well as those helping them in the process."

—*Dr. Eugene R. Seeloff*
Director, Career Planning and Placement Services
Lehigh University

"The book contains everything anybody would ever want to know about getting hired and beyond."

—*Steve D. Vanek*
Coordinator of Placement and Cooperative Education
Michigan Technological University

"I highly recommend it to the job seeker who wants to benefit from an inside view of the hiring process."

—*Charles J. Doherty*
Director of Placement
Moravian College

". . . .a book I wish I had written."

—*Richard A. Stewart*
Director, University Placement Service
Purdue University

How You Really
Get Hired

How You Really Get Hired

THE INSIDE STORY FROM A COLLEGE RECRUITER

John L. LaFevre

Director, Human Resources
Caradco Corporation

An Arco Book
Published by Prentice Hall Press
New York, New York 10023

An Arco Book
Published by Prentice Hall Press
A Division of Simon & Schuster, Inc.
Gulf+Western Building
One Gulf+Western Plaza
New York, New York 10023

PRENTICE HALL PRESS is a trademark of Simon & Schuster, Inc.

Manufactured in the United States of America

1   2   3   4   5   6   7   8   9   10

Library of Congress Cataloging-in-Publication Data

LaFevre, John L.
    How you really get hired.

    "An Arco book."
    1. Job hunting.   I. Title.
HF5382.7.L34   1986   650.1'4   86-18100
ISBN 0-13-431156-6 (Paper Edition)

To Pat, Amy, and Lori

CONTENTS

ACKNOWLEDGMENTS

There are three people in my life, who each in his own way, contributed to the management philosophy and personal business ethic that is reflected in this work.

Dr. Michael P. Soltys taught me how to interview and recruit and solidified my heart's feelings regarding the supreme value of human resources; a company's most valuable asset.

Colonel Roger A. Frey (ret. USAF), fostered and developed leadership and decision-making skills by letting me walk out on many limbs. His wisdom and kindness deeply affected my life.

John P. Mikulak is an unusual company president in that he truly recognizes the importance of each individual in the workforce. He gave me the freedom and authority to execute our common management philosophy at Caradco Corporation. It has been my privilege to work with these gentlemen and friends.

This page would not be complete without acknowledging three other special people who supported my efforts to write this book. Amy and Lori, daughters and all around nice human beings, have always been an inspiration. My wife, Pat, watched the kids and fed Whiskers many times even though it was my turn. Her tremendous patience, support, and understanding is embedded among these pages.

Introduction

This may be the most unusual job search book you'll ever read because its clarity, candor, and depth will take you right to the core of the job search process. If you have to be told that you need to have highly polished shoes and a firm handshake in an interview, this book is probably not for you. You'll find no basic, sugar-coated rhetoric on these pages.

This book is for serious job seekers ranging from high school students and college graduates to upper-level managers who want to become *experts* in the job search process. I offer a guarantee that this book will hurt your feelings, get you angry, make you laugh, and raise your eyebrows—but it will also teach you how to find and land the job you want.

I have interviewed thousands of young men and women for positions ranging from production worker to upper-level manager. I have interviewed on major college campuses across the country including Penn State, Columbia, Cal-Tech, Stanford, University of Toledo, Michigan, and Purdue, and the list goes on. That is me . . . the interviewer whom you are scheduled to meet next week for dinner at the company's headquarters, or in a campus cubbyhole office.

By now you may have read many books and articles about job searching written by social scientists and self-proclaimed experts. Placement officials, teachers, counselors, professors, relatives, and friends have all offered advice. It is time you heard my side of the story.

1

What You Must Know About Personnel And The Birth of A Job

1.1 INTRODUCTION

You do not have to be a doctor in order to successfully deliver a baby. In fact, many taxicab drivers in New York City will tell you firsthand that it can be done. It could certainly be argued, though, that an obstetrician who is knowledgeable about the entire physiological process leading to birth is much more likely to deliver a baby successfully than a New York City cabbie.

Similarly, a job seeker does not *have* to understand all of the steps leading to an approved job opening—how job specifications are developed, and how job salaries are determined. Like the cab driver, you could get by with luck and a lot of anxiety, *but a lack of understanding and knowledge of my business, personnel, decreases the likelihood of job search success and often is a direct factor in generating turndowns.* The purpose of this chapter is to help you become a job search specialist by learning the inside story of the personnel office and the job development process that eventually leads to the birth of an approved job opening. Knowledge of the procedural steps and considerations that occur *before* an ad is ever placed or a recruiting visit to a college campus is scheduled will help you understand the philosophy behind this book and will arm you with a tremendous competitive edge over other job seekers.

You are advised to set aside your idealism and put on a hard hat as we take a walk into the world of personnel administration and examine the birth of a job. Welcome to my jungle.

1.2   EMPLOYEES: A COSTLY AND RISKY INVESTMENT

The foundation of your job search strategy must include the understanding that an employee is the most costly and complex asset of a company. An employer must dip into company profit to *pay* for medical coverage, training, educational reimbursement programs, career development programs, savings plan, vacation, stock options, bonus, work space, company car, phone, travel expenses, pension, relocation, and a host of other benefits that are usually expected and sometimes demanded by employees. Oh yes, and salary. In addition to those direct-cost items, employees want challenge, opportunity for advancement, quality of work-life, jobs for spouses, and, quite often, the geographic location of their choice. (I won't even mention parking spaces, paid time off, child-care centers, employee associations, jogging tracks, and flextime.) To make matters even more difficult, we have no choice but to hire a human being as a "complete package," including personal problems ranging from alcoholism to marital strife that can decrease productivity. *Employees are expensive, very expensive.*

If an employee's work output does not offset the cost of the items above, he is, in effect, contributing to a loss. Companies, then, are forced to view employees as investments that must provide a reasonable return. As a job candidate, *you must prove that you offer the potential of a strong ROI* (return on investment).

Although every new hire is a real gamble, recent college graduates and job seekers making career changes are especially high-risk investments. They are "unknowns" and often require extensive training before the company can begin to reap the ROI. This fact helps explain the selectivity, careful evaluation, and comprehensive secondary (plant trip) interviews that often require as much as two full days to complete. The company must closely analyze the potential investment.

Many companies take the analysis even further by offering special employment programs for high school and college students such as co-op employment, summer employment, internships, and work-study programs. You see them advertised and marketed as developmental opportunities for students. The participants receive a paid work experience, the company receives great press in the community and on campus, but most important, the company is afforded the opportunity to scrutinize a possible investment: you.

When a company must make a business decision necessary to maintain or improve profit, hiring an employee is often the least attractive option to exercise. *Your job search strategy must address the fact that you are a high-cost/high-risk investment.* Later chapters offer practical tools to accomplish this critically important task.

You may be cringing just a bit at the idea of being treated as an investment first and a human being second, but the plain truth is that stockholders are interested in dividends and profits. Sugar-coated recruiters and artificially flavored job search books serve up mounds of romantic illusions of self-fulfillment and the wonderfulness of employment, but the real bottom line is what you can do to make the company more profitable. That basic premise should be incorporated into every job search activity from resume to interview. Don't make the mistake of walking into an interview with ME GENERATION boldly printed on your forehead. Get the offer before worrying about "me."

1.3   A NEED ARISES

The genesis of an approved job opening occurs when something happens that sends a signal called "deviation of workforce requirements." Following are a few common examples of such signals:

1.   George Smith, supervisor of purchasing, has just been

informed by his purchasing agent that the agent is quitting next week.

2. The annual manpower planning study has identified a need to hire five management trainees to replace three probable retirements in the next five years.

3. A promotion has created a vacancy in the advertising/brand management department.

4. A department reorganization has created the need for an assistant scheduler.

5. Our new facility will require 350 new hires. Develop a recruiting plan.

"Deviation of workforce requirements" signals are responded to differently in each situation depending on external and internal factors such as the economy, the company's strategic plan, the size of the company bureaucracy, the credibility and political power of the supervisor who generated the signal, and profit level.

For example, if the supervisor of purchasing has a weak power base in the company and is known always to complain about how he is shorthanded, approval to hire a management trainee may take up to a year! His request is placed on the company's proverbial back burner, which is the equivalent of a college student saying, "I think I'll get my car tuned up soon."

When the car finally refuses to move out on Interstate 80/94 and the V.P. of purchasing gets a phone call about an operation delay due to an order that was not expedited, two things happen. The car gets a tune-up and an ad for a purchasing trainee appears in the Sunday paper.

The time that elapses between "need to hire" and "published job opening" on average will be months, but the process can take up to a year. Chapter 3, Job Search Strategies, is entirely dedicated to teaching you how to find and land the purchasing agent job *before* the ad appears in the paper. Let's examine the steps that follow a "deviation of workforce requirements" signal.

1.4   JOB APPROVAL: A LONG AND WINDING ROAD

Approval to hire is a time-consuming process because a new hire is an expensive solution to a business problem. The length of time that it takes to get approval to hire correlates directly with the size of the company. Between each of the following steps, days and even weeks may go by:

1. Deviation of workforce requirements signal.

2. Try to make do—avoid hiring a new employee. Utilize overtime. Share responsibilities. Borrow someone from another department. Work smarter.

3. It isn't working. Document the need to the immediate boss.

4. The immediate boss offers ideas for avoiding having to add to force.

5. Send a follow-up letter or have another meeting with the boss.

6. Boss sends document outlining need to V.P. of department.

7. V.P. asks for complete job specification.

8. Approved by V.P., job specification is sent to personnel.

9. Salary administration determines salary range.

10. Personnel conducts search for candidates within the company (principle of promotion from within).

11. Personnel reviews current applications on file.

12. Personnel notifies state employment service to list job.

13. Personnel contacts local colleges; requests referrals.

14. Job advertisement, campus visit.

15. Initial screening of candidates, referrals to purchasing department.

16. Purchasing department interviews eight candidates. Makes offer.

17. New trainee is hired.

The extensive delay that occurs between the time when the initial need surfaces and the time when a job ad or a campus listing appears is a factor that should drive your entire job search strategy, because 80 percent of all job openings are filled before they are ever published on campus or listed in an advertisement. College students should recognize that only a minuscule fraction of all companies recruit on campus and out of those only a relative handful visit any one school. It is a ridiculous proposition to use a school's recruitment schedule as a primary job source. Such an approach is almost as absurd as using the Sunday want ads as the major job search tool. Chapter 3 offers a different strategy.

1.5　JOB SPECIFICATIONS: WHY YOU SHOULD IGNORE THEM

The excitement builds; Ameri-Can Company has a published job opening. You anxiously read the job specifications in the advertisement. After all, Ameri-Can is experiencing tremendous growth, has a great reputation, and you've heard that they are just an all-around great company. Your time has come, or so you thought. The job specification quickly transforms excitement into depression:

1. Ameri-Can only wants to interview mechanical engineers, not mechanical engineering *technologists*.

2. Ameri-Can requires a 3.0 G.P.A. and you only have a 2.85.

3. Ameri-Can will interview anyone except a liberal arts major.

4. Three years' experience required.

5. (fill in the blank) _____

You may think that job specifications are arbitrary, unfair, unreasonable, and illogical: *they often are*! We all know that there is not a statistically significant difference between a 2.85 and a 3.0 G.P.A. when applied in the context of a human being; and furthermore, a technology degree may require the *same* basic curriculum that a pure engineering degree required a few years ago! Why, then, do companies have such narrow job specifications in newspaper want ads and campus job postings? Pragmatic business logic is alive and well.

Good employers can arbitrarily be as picky as they want because of the laws of supply and demand. Your perception of fairness takes a back seat to pragmatism when arbitrary specifications are presented as "company standards." As demand increases to work for a company, the job specifications approach ridiculousness (LaFevre's Law of Specificity). Just try to get an interview with a Big Eight accounting firm! Besides requiring absolutely outstanding grades, candidates must document that they sleep in three-piece Brooks Brothers pajamas! Since almost all accounting majors dream of working for a Big Eight firm, the companies can specify an exact profile of the kind of candidate they will consider for employment (supply and demand). Such specifications minimize the selection gamble and improve the ROI at the expense of screening out many qualified candidates. (By the way, the preceding example is admittedly a slight exaggeration—two-piece pajamas are sometimes acceptable.)

Specifications are sometimes unintentionally narrow. In the purchasing department example, the job specification would probably have come directly from the supervisor. The supervisor receives a call from the personnel manager that might go something like this:

"Hello George? This is the personnel office calling. What kind of background are you looking for in that purchasing trainee position that was just approved?"

"Oh, I don't know. I guess a degree in business or a purchasing major—do they have purchasing majors?—would be good. I don't want a bookworm. A 'B' average would be OK. I'd appreciate it if you would move quickly to get some candidates because I'm in a real bind."

> **JOB POSTING: BOWLING GREEN UNIVERSITY**
> Purchasing Department Management Trainee, minimum 3.0 G.P.A., B.A. Bus., major in Procurement preferred, U.S. citizenship required. Send resume to Director of Personnel, Ameri-Can Company.

The important point is that Mr. Smith would probably *accept* a liberal arts major with strong communication skills, or a candidate with a 2.85 G.P.A., but those job seekers almost never become candidates because they screen themselves out. *Don't let arbitrary job specifications control your career options.*

If you really want to interview with Ameri-Can Company even though you don't meet the specifications, implement the following plan of action:

1. Thoroughly investigate the company by reading the literature in the college placement office or public library, requesting an annual report, or calling a sales office or manufacturing facility to learn about future plans and products. Get the name and title of the purchasing department manager and send a great cover letter and resume in application for the position. *Ignore the specifications!*

2. If the position is clearly associated with a particular department, call up the company's general switchboard and ask to be connected to the vice president's office or manager/supervisor of that department. When the secretary answers the phone, simply state that you are sending a letter to his or her boss and would like to confirm the spelling of his or her name and title. Send a letter with attached resume *describing your interest in the company, using specific company information that only a person who*

Sample Letter for Bypassing Campus Job Specifications

Ms. Diane Christmas
4526 Elizabeth Lane
Chicago, Illinois 60610
312-666-6666 (Bus.)
March 22, 1986

Mr. George Smith
Sypervisor of Purchasing
Ameri-Can Company
Cantree Center
Toledo, Ohio 25444

Dear Mr. Smith:

This letter and enclosed resume is submitted in application for the position of Management Trainee in the Purchasing Department. I am a senior at Northwestern University majoring in Liberal Arts with a heavy curriculum emphasis in business communications and analysis.

Your annual report indicates that Ameri-Can's operating capacity rate is expected to increase to 85% by the end of the third quarter, which must impact directly on the purchasing function. My successful experience as a shipment coordinator has taught me that such a fast-paced environment requires a detail- and results-oriented individual who can be counted on to get the job done in a timely and efficient manner. I am an innovative, resourceful team-player who learns quickly and who knows the meaning of hard work. I have paid for 80% of my education by working year-round. I offer that same drive and dedication to my new employer.

Your Mr. Tom Sully, Chicago sales office, has advised me that the purchasing function is computerized. I offer a strong background as an experienced user of my own personal computer which will facilitate my ability to quickly adapt to your Purch/Con System and immediately begin contributing to the department.

Since your job posting specified business majors only, I can only sign up for an interview with your permission. I respectfully request the opportunity to meet with your representative on campus next week. Thank you for your consideration. I anxiously await your reply.

Sincerely,

Ms. Diane Christmas

has done extensive research would have. Mention in the letter that you know Ameri-Can is coming to campus to interview and you would really appreciate the opportunity to interview, but since you do not meet the specifications special permission would be required. Vice presidents and managers are more impressed by business drive than by G.P.A. Approval to interview will most likely follow. If it is impossible to determine the V.P.'s or department head's name and title, proceed to number 3.

3. Send a letter similar to the one just described directly to the interviewer (correct name and title mandatory) who is coming to campus. After proving your sincere interest, tell the recruiter that you would be willing to meet at the hotel, at lunch, or in the morning before the regular interviews begin. It would be a big plus if you could drop someone's name, such as the sales manager that you called previously—prove your sincere interest. Recruiters are always on the run, so don't wait for his response. Tell the interviewer that you will call next week to see if an interview can be arranged. Thank him ahead of time for giving you the opportunity to discuss a career opportunity with Ameri-Can. In my years as a recruiter, I have never turned down such a request. I should also add that rarely are such requests received, because *most job seekers simply allow the specifications to screen them out.*

The same procedure applies to bypassing specifications of newspaper job ads. Ignore the fact that the ad states that you must have three years' experience. That requirement was probably created by a quick phone call to the department head who said, "I'd just as soon have someone who has had a couple of years' experience." *Understand job specifications for what they are: arbitrary, biased, off-the-wall requirements generated by a business's pragmatic need to screen out a large portion of the job seeker pool. If you are really interested in a company, don't let them screen you out so easily.* Be a fighter; be persistent.

At this point in their reading, college placement officials' hearts are beating violently because job specifications are a real sore point and something of a sacred cow. In the interest of their health and my safety I had better reduce the rate of blood flow. Placement officials cannot allow a student on a college interview schedule if he does not meet the job specifications. Such an action would endanger the recruiting relationship with the company. Don't ever ask the placement office to bypass the specification by allowing you on the schedule and don't ever sneak on the schedule unless you are interviewing with the CIA. Some schools and companies will allow candidates who do not meet the specifications to get on the schedule if there is a vacant time slot. Such an approach implies that since the recruiter has nothing better to do he may as well interview you— a very unimpressive and nonproductive strategy. If you want an interview, work for it. Don't screen yourself out.

1.6   THE PERSONNEL FUNCTION: WHY WE ARE SO SLOW

A personnel office is a hectic, fast-paced place with ringing phones, meetings, interviews, flashing word processors, and reams of paperwork flowing through a complex network of policies and procedures. It is a Grand Central Station of people moving in and out to get hired, fired, tested, laid off, or reinstated from a leave; to return from a pregnancy; to raise complaints, questions, and concerns; to receive counseling; to change a name, address, or beneficiary; and on and on. Typical business functions performed include training, management development, testing, manpower planning, college relations, recruitment, benefit administration, affirmative action, medical administration, labor relations, salary administration, and employment policy administration.

Now pause for a moment to reflect on to a different image.

Picture a single resume or a single interview evaluation quietly observing all of the frenzy and crisis activity, peeking out from the middle of a large stack of papers held down by a sack lunch with a banana sticking out at the top. Personalize that image because I am talking about *your* resume or *your* interview evaluation. The lunch bag is eventually removed, the banana is eaten, and the stack of papers is processed, but not nearly as expeditiously as you would wish. Other more critical business priorities constantly bump your file to "hold" status.

Meanwhile, back in countless dorms and households, job seekers turn to friends and spouses and say:

"I interviewed with them over four weeks ago and still haven't heard a thing. Do you think I should call the personnel office or will that just reduce my chances of getting an offer?"

"I answered the ad seven weeks ago and they didn't even bother to send a turndown. I guess I was ruled out."

"She told me I would hear back in four weeks. The interview really went well. I wonder what happened?"

You can expect to feel a sense of helplessness during the waiting period following an interview on the mailing of an application or resume. Following are suggested actions that may serve to alleviate the anxiety and actually improve your odds of getting an offer:

At the end of an interview always ask when you can expect to hear back from the company and in what manner the notification will be given—letter or phone. Most interviewers will almost always give an optimistic time frame. (Three weeks sounds at least reasonable; eight weeks sounds a little embarrassing.) *As you are waiting for a response, keep in mind that companies are much more punctual with turndowns than with offers.* As soon as a candidate is screened out, the file is given to a clerk who sends out standard turndown letters with wonderful efficiency. There is some comfort and a lot of truth in the statement "No news is good news."

Never call a recruiter or personnel office before the indicated review time period has elapsed without a good reason. The fact that you are impatient, excited, and anxious is not a good reason. Following are two examples of legitimate calls that should be made:

1. "Hello, Mr. Jablonski? This is Mark Canton calling. I am the

M.E. graduate you interviewed at West Virginia University on April 8. You may recall that I am the student who organized the Kenny Rogers concert on campus and we talked about your interest in country music. [NOTE: It is important whenever calling a recruiter that you always identify yourself so that the recruiter can *really* remember who you are. He may have interviewed 150 M.E.'s since his meeting with you.] You mentioned in our interview that it would take four to six weeks for my file to go through the channels. It has only been five weeks since our interview, but I am calling to let you know that I have completed the requirements for my degree and will be leaving for home tomorrow. May I give you my new address and phone number? By the way, since we met I have received a copy of your most recent annual report and have discussed the offerings of the Nashville area with the chamber of commerce. I am really excited about the possibility of employment with AmeriCan and I can honestly say that your company is one of my top choices."

2."Hello, Mr. Carter? This is James Keller calling. I am the marketing major you interviewed on March 12. You may recall we discussed how my proficiency in French might tie in with your newly acquired subsidiary in France. I am calling because I am in somewhat of a dilemma. I am holding an offer from another company with a deadline to respond by next Friday. Quite honestly, your company is a high priority on my list, and I'm hoping that consideration of my application can be expedited. If necessary, I could request an extension of the deadline on my other offer, but I thought I would call you first to get a feel for the current status of my file."

After the company-indicated time frame for review has elapsed, call to request your status. Many candidates are hesitant to do this, thinking that the call might be viewed as harassment or "bugging." On the contrary, a phone call is a compliment to the company and the recruiter. It is a solid indicator of interest. Be positive. Don't start out your call by saying, "I'm calling to check on the status of my file. You told me it would take four to six weeks and it has now been seven weeks so I thought I'd better call." That statement implies that the recruiter either lied, is inefficient, or lost the file. Putting a company on the defensive is not a way to score points. Remember the lunch bag with the banana sticking out. Call because you are really interested in the company, *not* because you haven't heard from them:

"Hello, Mr. Callahan? This is Joan Baker calling. You may recall that I am the business major from Moravian College whom you interviewed on May 12—we discussed how we both vacation at Cape May. I am calling to request the status of my job application. Since our interview I have discussed Ameri-Can's sales training program with Mr. Sully, of your Chicago sales office, and I am even more excited about the opportunity and challenge that your 2-2-2 program offers."

Your personal priority to gain employment ranks number one on your list, but is ranked considerably lower on the company's priorities. Frustration and even anger are commonplace as job seekers anxiously await the phone call or religiously meet the mailman each day. As you read this book, you'll notice that I advocate employing a sense of humor in the rejection-laden process of the job search, but there is no joke here. The anxiety is real and the pain of waiting for your future via a phone call from a stranger somehow seems absurd. Deal with our "slowness" by accepting it as one of the rules of the game. Remember the image of the crisis-oriented personnel office and expect to wait longer than anticipated. We will not change.

1.7 EVERYTHING YOU NEED TO KNOW ABOUT SALARY ADMINISTRATION

The salary administration section of a personnel office has filing cabinets filled with salary surveys, charts, job rating scales, comparable worth analyses, and a standard operating procedure guide, all of which are used to determine a salary *range* for any given position. The methodology is not important. As a job seeker you only need to know that a salary range exists for virtually every position.

Companies know what the market is paying and decide exactly where they want their offers to fit within the range. There are a number of sophisticated salary negotiation maneuvers, but they are not really appropriate for lower-middle management and entry-level job seekers. Negotiation of stock options, perks, scheduled salary increases, and employment contracts is reserved for middle management and above. Your salary negotiation should consist of a single strategy and action plan: *After you receive an offer, ALWAYS ask for more money.*

There is a certain level of discomfort associated with this task, but you have nothing to lose and a lot to gain. If you receive just $75 per month more as a result of your request, a simple calculation says that over ten years you make $9,000 plus interest. Not a bad return for a brief moment of anxiety! *No company that you would want to work for would ever rescind an offer because you attempted to negotiate the salary offer.* Quite the opposite; negotiation is a sign of maturity and is viewed positively if handled correctly. Caution: Don't be pushy or egotistically threatening; you are not negotiating from a position of strength. Use the following example as a representative approach:

"Hello? Mr. Jackson? This is Bill Veith. I received your offer a few days ago and to say I am excited about the opportunity to work for Ameri-Can is an understatement. As we discussed in the interview, the position is a perfect match for my own career goals. You requested that I formally respond to the offer by May 18 and I expect to have no problem meeting that date. I do have one question for you, though. I have investigated the housing costs in Houston and have found that housing is quite a bit more expensive than in the Midwest. Would it be possible to have the offer increased a little to compensate for the housing differential? Your offer is competitive, but a little extra would really meet my financial needs at this time. If your offer is not negotiable, I will certainly understand."

How can I, as a recruiter, get upset with you? Housing *is* expensive in Houston. You were polite, sincere, and diplomatic.

I certainly would not withdraw your offer because of such a phone call. Remember, at this point I *want* you to come to work at Ameri-Can. I might just add $75 per month to the offer to improve our chances of gaining your acceptance. *After receiving the offer, always ask for more money.* You have absolutely nothing to lose.

I should add a caveat dedicated to all of those idealistic candidates who say that the starting salary is not important; the stockholders and I say, "Thank you." At the risk of overstating my point, let me conclude with an ancient Chinese saying: "Job fulfillment does not a Pontiac Fiero buy."

1.8   MANPOWER PLANNING

Since most trainee positions are generated by manpower planning studies, it is worthwhile to take a brief look at this process to understand better the nature of those job openings and of career development in general.

Manpower planning is based on statistical guesses about future turnover, probable retirements, possible retirements, projected business requirements, projected business climate, projected promotions, and other projected projections. (I personally would not travel on any bridge built with such a formula.) Manpower planning is not a science; at best it is a calculated guess based on all available data.

This fact has particular relevance for the entry-level job seeker, who often assumes that the company is seeking to fill a specific position with a specific career path. The narrowly defined specification for the job reinforces the misconception that the job is clearly delineated. As a result, job seekers often expect a far greater level of career development detail than is possible. A young engineer starting out in the design and development division might be just as likely to end up in another department and another facility as he is to head up the division in which he began his career.

As a job search specialist in an interview, you should request detailed information regarding responsibilities and accountability that you can expect in the *first two years*. You must have that information in order to prove that you have the skills and attributes required for the position. General questions about long-term career opportunities may be briefly addressed, but don't waste valuable interviewing time discussing what job you might have five or ten years from now. Statistically, there is a good chance that you won't even be working at that company in ten years.

It is something of a paradox that interviewers who have absolutely no idea in the world where you might be in ten years will often ask, "What are your long-term goals?" or, "What do you expect you'll be doing in five years?" Recruiters know that the validity of a response to such a crystal-ball question is nil—even short-term goals change dramatically when melded with work experience. The question simply serves as a tool for the interviewer to discover what you *really* want to do. Shielded by the perceived "safety" of such a futuristic question, job seekers often show their true colors, or worse, provide the recruiter with a reason to send a turndown. The following typical responses by interviewees illustrate my point:

Question: "What are your long-term goals?"
"I know that you require working on the shop floor for a year or two, but long-term I prefer working in an office environment as a manager."
(This candidate may not be a dyed-in-the-wool, hands-on engineer—TURNDOWN.)

"Long-term I would like to gain experience in your sales department and eventually move into public affairs or human resources."
(Companies generally hire salespeople who really love and want sales only—a special breed. This candidate's response has compromised his commitment to a sales career—TURNDOWN.)

As a job seeker you may be thinking, "Aw c'mon! Isn't that a little ridiculous and unfair to get a turndown based on an off-the-cuff response to a question?" Understand that your competitor for the sales position has a resume that looks exactly like yours except for the name at the top. He also was a varsity ballplayer and also achieved a 3.1 G.P.A. He responded to the same question as follows:

"First, I am really interested in sales as a career and plan to work my way up in the sales organization. I know that company needs and personal interests do change and I am flexible to adapt to wherever I can most contribute to company profit. The real bottom line is that long-term I hope to achieve the highest level in your company that my capabilities and potential allow."

In this response, commitment to sales is reinforced, vocational maturity and flexibility to adapt are presented, and the goal of having a positive impact on company profit is noted. The recruiter will select the candidate whose responses in total indicate the best gamble for a high return on investment.

Manpower planning is a calculated projection (business terminology for "guess") of future staffing requirements. Don't ask or expect to know what you might be doing in five or ten years. Job specifications are based on the initial assignments expected in the first few years. Don't spend valuable interviewing time proving that you'll be great in upper management; prove that you can successfully contribute to the company's short-term needs if you want to land a job offer.

1.9 HOW COMPANIES DECIDE TO VISIT OR BYPASS YOUR COLLEGE

There are literally thousands of accredited colleges and universities in the United States and Canada. Understanding the criteria used by companies to decide which schools to visit and which to bypass offers a unique insight into and perspective on the employment selection process. The decision to visit a college is based on the evaluation and analysis of defined criteria. Companies look for the best ROI for recruitment dollars. A college recruitment itinerary is a business decision. Following are typical considerations that may lead to a decision to recruit at your school:

Past Recruitment Record. How many hires per year for the last five years? Each school is charted and ranked according to productivity of hires. Success breeds success, and every company has certain "bread-and-butter" schools.

Geographic Proximity to Business Location. Forget for a moment that all job seekers are trained to say, "Yes, I am open for relocation." Analysis proves that the relationship of geographic location of work assignment and geographic location of home are jointly a significant recruitment factor. A company location that allows a trip home for a three-day weekend is a general rule of thumb. I mean, can you picture a Columbia University grad from New York City riding a horse to work in Butte, Montana? Maybe, but companies will bet that a Montana graduate will be a much happier rider and employee.

General Academic Competitiveness. There is a quality of education associated with every institution. *Lovejoy's College Guide* and *Barron's Profiles of American Colleges* are standard references that are used to evaluate the quality and competitiveness of colleges and universities. Visit your library, examine these reference books, and see how your school stacks up. Data such as major programs of study, enrollment figures, median SAT and ACT scores of freshmen, and college admission selector ratings point toward level of quality. The status of the school's name and its general reputation also carry weight. The faculty at a small Northern Wisconsin high-caliber school could certainly challenge the validity of such analysis, but if you examine their recruiting schedule my point is made.

Minority Population. Affirmative action is an important social, ethical, and legal consideration. In order to hire minorities, companies simply must visit schools that have a significant minority population.

Profile of Student Population. A student body has a personality of its own. It's an intangible intuitive factor that is at least partially based on factual data. For example, one college has all male students and a significant percentage of them are first-time college students in their families. Many students overcame difficult odds to break the family education barrier and could be categorized as hard-working fighters. On the other hand, another school has a student body comprised of third-generation students with hands callused from sailing on the Cape. Companies match their own "personality" or the kind of job candidate required for a position with the perceived personality of the school. You may jokingly refer to your college as a "party school," but companies are not smiling. Now, before you shift your position on the couch, let me say that graduates in glass dorms should not cast stones. You judge companies with the same unfair stereotypes.

Specific Curriculum.   Companies will recruit at a school based on the reputation of a specific department. Your professor's reputation or lack of one can count your school in or out.

Political Factors.   Wherever Lee Iacocca received his degree, you can bet that Chrysler is recruiting there. Fortunately for the Chrysler recruiting team, he graduated from a fine institution, Lehigh University. Alma maters of key executives are almost always on the recruiting itinerary.

The preceding considerations have important meaning for job seekers. Allow your understanding of the criteria to affect your job search strategy. If you are seeking employment with a heavy-industry manufacturer, sell your school's reputation as a producer of practical, hard-working engineers. If a high-tech company is bypassing your college because it is in a small town in Northern Wisconsin, use your professor's applicable research and reputation to your advantage. If your school is geographically located near a company's facility, use that fact to your advantage.

Conversely, if your school's competitive ranking, reputation, geographic location, or personality is a *liability* that will prevent your being considered by a certain company, you must recognize that fact and face it head-on by using the tools offered in Chapter 7, "How to Handle Liabilities in an Interview."

Conclusion

The key to effective job search is to become a job search specialist, because companies make offers to those who best present themselves in the employment selection process, not necessarily to those who are most qualified for the job. A highly qualified candidate with weak job search skills cannot successfully compete against a job search specialist. Unfair as that may be, it is the only game in town.

Understanding the birth of a job does not make you a specialist, but it does firmly plant your foot in a new direction, and has already separated you from your competition. The purpose of the rest of this book is to widen the gap and give you a competitive edge.

Important Points to Remember
1. You must prove that you offer the potential of a strong ROI.

2. An employee is the most costly and complex asset of a company.

3. Interviewers want to know what you can do to make the company more profitable.

4. Most jobs are filled before ever becoming published openings.

5. Don't let job specifications screen you out.

6. Remember the lunch bag and banana. Be patient. Expect slowness.

7. No news from a potential employer is generally good news. We are fast with turndowns, slow with offers.

8. Graduating from your particular school offers certain strengths and liabilities. Recognize both in your job search strategy.

2

How To Select Companies That Meet Your Career Needs

2.1 INTRODUCTION

Before addressing the subject of how to find job openings and how to answer ads, etc., it is important that you gain a general understanding of *how to determine the competitive business posture and future outlook of potential employing industries and companies.* To say, "I want to work in a growth industry or with a big Fortune 100 company" sounds great, but what are the career advantages and disadvantages associated with growth industries and big old conglomerates? A big company in a mature industry may offer great training programs and benefits, but may also be slow to hand out responsibilities. Will that company meet your needs? Do you want to work in an entrepreneurial, fast-paced environment or a heavily structured and traditional environment? Different strokes for different folks, but the important point is that you should recognize what you're getting into to make sure that the industry and company can meet your personal and career needs.

To make a valid career decision to work in a particular industry or for a particular company requires that you analyze the information provided in standard industry publications and annual reports. It is important to identify the current posture and competitive position of a potential employer and the future outlook for his industry because when you join a company your future happiness and success is, without a doubt, linked to the company's current strategy and competitive position in the marketplace and the future trends of the industry. You may be a great employee, but if the company files for bankruptcy or begins eliminating excessive layers of management, your career could go right down the drain. If, for example, you join an industry that is being killed by substitute product(s)—as, for example, plastic is replacing steel, your career will most certainly be affected. It is a valid decision to join the young satellite television dish industry only if you realize the potential risks and rewards, and it may be a catastrophic career mistake to seek a long-term career with a "mature" company that is losing a significant market share each year.

No one can guarantee the future, but you *can* minimize your career risk and enhance the possibility of achieving your goals by performing a gross competitive analysis of your potential employer and the current state of his industry. Controlling your career begins by considering industries and employers in those industries that can meet your needs for the next five years or so (you'll probably be working somewhere else by then). *You need to know up front what kind of business scenario you're walking into when you accept a job offer.* This chapter lays out a simple general framework for industry and company analysis. It will help answer two important questions as you explore your career options:

1. "Will this particular industry help meet my career goals?"

2. "Will this particular company meet my personal and career needs?"

2.2 DESIGNER JEANS AND DESIGNER COMPANIES

Our society and its love affair with status has created hundreds of designer products ranging from jeans to underwear that are purchased, at least in part, because of the status associated with owning or wearing the product. We are conditioned to seek the status of designer clothing, shampoo, cars, perfume, and *designer companies.* For accountants, the status of working for a "Big Eight" accounting company becomes obvious when trying to secure an interview. Everyone wants a designer accounting firm and the price paid for the "label" shows in terms of dramatically increased competition for the job. The fifteenth or twenty-second largest accounting firm may offer much better opportunities for achieving your goals. Don't screen companies out because they don't have a status address or logo. IBM does not necessarily spell happiness and fulfillment. A little-known high-tech growth company may offer tremendous visibility and opportunity.

The transition of American business from big conglomerates to smaller, more flexible producers is an important consideration in your job search strategy. Our new "world economy" is breeding hundreds of smaller, specialized companies that quickly seize opportunities and also quickly redirect focus when the market changes. Such companies can offer the immediate challenges, experience, and rewards that you are seeking. The bottom line: Don't be constrained by image and status. Explore a wide parameter of career opportunities with many different industries and companies, including the smaller and lesser-known companies that will take on a more important role in the eighties.

2.3 ANALYZING INDUSTRY POSTURE

Industries work their way through a standard life cycle that includes four stages:

Stage 1. Birth
Stage 2. Growth
Stage 3. Maturity
Stage 4. Death

Industry progression through each of the stages can take more than your lifetime or just a few years. For example, the computer industry has been in the growth stage for *decades,* while the steel industry matured in the seventies and will most likely remain in that stage for decades to come. Industries can mature practically overnight due to a shift in consumer attitude (video game industry) or technological advancements (steam engine industry). There are career pros and cons associated with joining an industry in any of the stages. As a job seeker you had better know what they are. Don't cop out by saying that only the job itself is important, because you can find a similar job in many different industries and companies. Potential advancement, mobility, visibility, quality of life, pay, and other important career factors are directly related to industry and company posture. You have a choice.

Stage 1: Birth A new industry is a relatively high-risk/high-reward employment situation because potential growth and marketplace acceptance of the product have not yet been established. For example, the video game industry offered high initial rewards but matured practically overnight. Many individuals accepted the high-risk gamble by joining the new industry only to find themselves laid off a few years later. A more successful gamble is exemplified by the new software development industry. That industry has successfully moved from birth to the growth stage. A few years ago, the cable television network industry was a high-risk/high-return gamble that also has paid off well for many individuals who joined that fledgling industry. Will the satellite television dish industry survive and grow? Will the videocassette industry survive and offer long-term career challenges and opportunities? Will biogenetics be legislated into nonexistence? The potential rewards of joining a fledgling industry are great, but you should recognize the high risk. A young college graduate with few financial and personal commitments may relish the unique challenges inherent in a new industry. There is a lot to be said for the excitement of working in a ground-floor, fast-paced, unstructured, creative work environment where potential rewards are high. If you can afford the gamble, a new industry might be your cup of tea. New industries need entrepreneurs who are driven to work hard long hours to succeed. On the other hand, if you are seeking a formally structured training program, long-term employment, and a more traditional package of benefits (e.g., vision care, dental coverage), a new industry will probably not serve your needs.

Stage 2: Growth   Growth industries offer the most balanced career opportunities because new challenges, visibility, and potential high rewards are presented along with relative security and stability. Expansions, new facilities, expanding markets, technological product enhancements, and a sales revenue increasing at an annual rate of 8 percent or more are typical growth industry indicators. Growth industries such as computers and synthetic materials offer low-risk, relatively stable employment and high opportunities and rewards. That combination of benefits makes growth industries a clear choice for many job seekers, which in turn means higher job competition. Landing a job in a growth industry requires absolutely outstanding job search skills, outstanding qualifications, entrepreneurial spirit, and an ability to work in a demanding, fluid environment that is evolving and searching for structure.

Stage 3: Maturity   A mature industry is one in which sales have levelled through the years and are now growing slightly or about the same rate as the general economy. Companies in a mature industry are often established and firmly entrenched in a certain niche or segment of the market. For example, Maytag Corporation holds a share of the high-quality appliance market while other appliance manufacturers in the industry have established market shares in the low-price segment. *Traditional values and a conservative environment are often indicative of companies in a mature industry.* (Maytag has used the same guy in their commercials for the last two hundred years!) Companies in mature industries often integrate backwards to facilitate reducing prices in order to compete. For example, an appliance company could integrate backwards by purchasing a metals processing company or an electric motor company. Mature companies often have to compete on price, and backward integration helps reduce the total cost of delivering the product. The advantages of working for a company in a mature industry include good benefits, highly structured organizational environment, and controlled career development programs. Risks include downscaling of operations (layoffs), and reorganizations in a negative, low morale environment. Entrepreneurs are often frustrated in mature industries because "Don't rock the boat" is still a motto in some corporate handbooks.

As a job seeker you should also be aware that mature industries are ripe for substitution of products. In the appliance industry, for example, new electrolytic cleaning systems that electrically charge the dirt, stains, and grease may someday replace the antiquated "water and detergent" cleaning machines. Examples of substitute products include:

1. Word processors replacing typewriters

2. Plastic replacing steel

3. Film discs replacing film rolls

4. Inexpensive 35mm cameras replacing instamatics

5. Digital devices replacing analog devices

6. Synthetic fabrics replacing natural fabrics

7. Microwave ovens replacing electric and gas ranges

If you decide to join a company that is in the mature stage (manufacturing typewriters, for example), recognize the risks and the rewards. A mature company may be your best match because you desire a formal training program, or it may be a terrible match because you seek creative and entrepreneurial freedom. A mature company will often choose to diversify into other industries. Diversification can open promotional doors and increase potential mobility. Don't be immature by *just* looking for a good job. Find a good job with a company in an industry that can meet your career needs. Be in control of your life by making an informed, logical career decision.

Stage 4: Death Industries proceed to the death stage when substitute products wipe out the market. Companies in dying industries will follow suit unless they diversify or restructure to hold a market niche. For example, even though the market for analog clock (clocks with hands) has been largely replaced by digital clocks, kitchen wall clocks are still a niche market for analog. For some unknown reason, consumers still prefer an analog clock hanging next to the ceramic apple in the kitchen. An analog clock manufacturer's strategy, then, could be to enter the digital market, close down analog facilities entirely, or simply downsize operations and hang on to the kitchen wall-clock niche. As a job candidate considering employment with a clock manufacturer, you need to understand the significance of the current and future outlook for the industry. What is the company's strategy for survival? Helping a company in a dying industry survive is a tremendous challenge with extremely high risks. If you pull it off, you could write a book and go on *The Phil Donahue Show*, but if you fail, Merv Griffin won't even talk to you.

To determine the life cycle stage of an industry is not very difficult. Use resources such as (1) annual reports, (2) industry journals (see your librarian for help), (3) sales catalogs, (4) acquaintances or relatives who work in the industry, (5) business professors, (6) placement counselors, (7) Moody's Index, (8) Dun & Bradstreet's listing, and (9) magazine articles. Answer the following questions:

1. What are the future trends of the industry?

2. Are sales increasing significantly, levelling off, or declining?

3. Are substitute products appearing in the market?

4. Are imports hurting market share? (Sign of maturity.)

5. Are companies in the industry bailing out via diversification? (Maturity.)

6. Is the industry expanding or are companies downsizing operations?

7. Does the product represent a new technology? (Birth.)

8. Are new companies entering the market? (Growth.)

Industry Life Cycle vs. Job Environment (Figure 1)

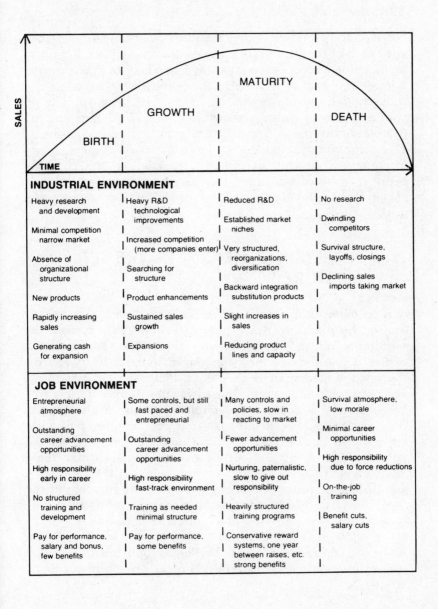

Summary

There are career advantages and disadvantages associated with each of the industry life stages. If you are planning to attend graduate school at night at the University of Chicago with a long-term goal of moving to the Southwest, then a mature industry with a company in the Chicago suburbs would meet your needs by providing a structured training program and tuition reimbursement in a traditional nine-to-five environment. That same company would not serve the needs of a young entrepreneur who wants maximum responsibility and accountability in a non-traditional, fast-paced environment. *Career planning and control begins now, not on the first day you report to work.*

2.4   ANALYZING THE COMPANY'S POSTURE

After determining the industry life cycle stage, you must examine the position of the potential employing companies within the industry. Using the same information sources listed earlier, determine who the major players in the industry are and the relative market share they hold. Plotting a company's record of profits on a graph (based on the company's last five years' results) will present a simplistic picture of the company's current and future outlook. Your goal is not to perform a complicated business analysis, but rather to get a feel for the company's strategy and future growth possibilities. Use a common-sense approach to determine whether the company's posture meets your needs. For example, if the company is the fifteenth largest manufacturer in a mature industry that is downsizing, you could assume it offers rather bleak career opportunities unless its product, quality, or service is uniquely identified in comparison with the larger companies. Generally a company will market its products using one of three general strategies:

1.   Low price

2. Quality/service

3. Differentiation (product is perceived by the consumer as different)

Get answers to the following questions either before or during an interview and you'll have a good feel for whether the company can facilitate your career and personal goals (these are great questions to have in your back pocket during the interview):

1   What are the product lines and market shares?

2. Who are the major competitors?

3. Is the company emphasizing price, quality, service, or differentiation? (Do you think that strategy will work?)

4. Is the company dependent on a small number of major customers? (This would be a risky situation—loss of a major customer means layoffs.)

5. Does the company have a broad base of customers?

6. Is the company the technology leader in its industry or does it follow others?

7. Is the company losing or gaining market share? Why?

8. When was the last time the company opened a new office or built a new facility?

9. Are there any new entrants to the market, e.g., foreign suppliers?

10. What is the track record of profits over the past five years?

11. What is the company's basic competitive strategy for the future?

NOTE: Large conglomerates are often active in a number of industries. Divisions of such large corporations should be analyzed as if they were separate companies.

2.5   PUBLIC AND PRIVATE COMPANIES

Public companies are controlled by independent boards which make broad business decisions to serve the stockholders. Pragmatic business logic is the rule of thumb. As an employee in a public company, you will be rewarded for your contributions to profit. Politics and luck are factors in being promoted, but competency and achievements play the key role in determining your future. I am biased, but I suggest that private companies are much more political in nature.

Private companies are often controlled by "Grandpa," and it is no stroke of coincidence that there are a lot of people with the same last name in the company phone book. Key positions are often handed out to relatives as family heirlooms. Such an environment is paternalistic, political, and generally autocratic, not participative. I know there are exceptions, but I caution you to examine the phone book and the decision-making climate before linking up with a family enterprise. Disregard this section if you are planning to marry "Grandpa's" niece or nephew; in fact, disregard this book—you won't need it.

2.6   BIG VERSUS SMALL

There are many career trade-offs involved in working for a big company rather than a small company. Again, required on your part is an inventory of your career and personal needs to match against each employment scenario. For the purposes of my discussion, I'll define "big" as a multi-facility company having at least two thousand employees. "Small" is defined as a single facility company or a multi-facility company having less than two thousand employees. The following statements are general observations intended to stimulate your own reflection and analysis.

Big Companies

Job Specialization   Entry-level and lower management positions in big companies are narrowly defined. For example, if you are hired into an entry-level position in human resources with a big company, you would most likely be placed in a narrow job function such as testing administrator, affirmative action coordinator, or labor relations trainee. For the first year or so of employment, you might spend 90 percent of your time handling discrimination complaints and tracking affirmative action programs—a very narrow function. This example applies pretty much across the board for entry-level jobs in big companies. The story you'll hear from recruiters for big companies is that you'll be moved or rotated through a variety of functional areas to provide good exposure, and that the first specialized assignment is just a starting point. What you're not told is that the moves will not come as often as you might like or as frequently as implied. Working in a specialized function creates a management constraint on moving you, because someone else then has to be transferred to your slot to pick up your duties. Also, some supervisors become very attached to good employees and may delay or even abort transfers. Big companies are apt to move slowly in effecting transfers.

Mobility   A large corporation will have more career path possibilities and broader opportunities for advancement than a small company. A marketing trainee, for example, could move into advertising, public affairs, planning, operations, or a host of other vacancies. Furthermore, a large company can search for promotional opportunities in other departments, subsidiaries, and even other companies under the corporate umbrella. Ideally, you should be promoted as soon as you are ready, but the drawback in small companies is that you can be ready before any positions are available.

Higher Salary Potential   A president of a small company who makes $50,000 per year makes less money than many mid-level managers in Fortune 100 companies. Company size directly correlates to salary. A manager of engineering in a large company will draw a higher salary than is paid for the equivalent position in a small company. Generally, big bucks are easier to find in big companies.

Exposure to State-of-the-Art Systems   Research facilities, laboratories, computer-aided manufacturing, and the latest technologies are more prevalent in big companies, which can afford the high cost of "state of the art." Small companies generally lag behind big companies in technology. Do you want to work on the cutting edge of technology with a big company, or would you enjoy helping a small company steal the latest technological advances and with a little bit of bailing wire, retrofit the technology to a vintage machine? Each scenario is exciting and each scenario requires a special kind of employee.

Better Benefits   Large companies will usually have better benefits than smaller companies—savings plans, tuition reimbursement, vision care, liberal vacations, company clubs, etc. Certainly, a job seeker should not base an employment decision on an insurance program deductible, but benefits should be considered as part of the company's total compensation package.

Small Companies

General Duties   In small companies, positions will usually have broader functional authority and higher responsibility. A purchasing trainee in a small company may represent 50 percent of his department, reporting directly to the manager of purchasing (the other 50 percent). A job seeker could join a small company as manager of safety and training and be responsible for the entire facility's safety and training programs. That same job seeker might join a Fortune 50 company as an assistant safety engineer in charge of fire safety for one division. Specialist versus generalist, it's your choice.

Visibility   Visibility is much higher in small companies. Handling a special project for the president of a small company can occur early in your career. In big companies, the closest you may get to the president is when you touch his picture in the corporation's annual report. Visibility and exposure in smaller companies make it easier to be recognized for contributions and effort.

Friendly Atmosphere   Smaller companies are more likely to have a friendly atmosphere. Team spirit and closeness, almost like that in a family, are nice benefits in many small companies.

Greater Opportunity to Affect the Organization   Your actions and contributions in a small company can significantly affect the organization, with visible results. The success of your project can affect profitability, and you can see the results. In a large company your assignment may be a small piece of a multi-million dollar project; you may never even understand the overall need and probably will not be closely associated with the final product. Do you want to build a house and then step back and take a look at the final product or can you be happy in a large company with an assignment to do the electrical wiring for the bathroom in the family room?

Conclusion

The driving point of this chapter is that you should consider certain industry and company factors when seeking to find a job and when considering job offers:

1.   The industry's life cycle stage

2.   Industry trends

3.   Company's competitive position

4.   Future outlook and strategy for the company

5.   Public versus private

6.   Big versus small

Determine your career needs and match them to the industry and the company. Analyze and understand the career advantages and disadvantages as they relate to you. You have a choice.

3

Job Search Strategies

3.1 INTRODUCTION

For millions of job seekers, the Sunday morning paper repre-
sents the primary source of job openings. Across the nation on
every Sunday morning, job seekers pore over the ads hoping
to find something that sounds like a great match. Each Sunday, thousands pin their dreams on that one job ad that sounds
almost too good to be true—a perfect match! Just drive by any
main post office on Sunday evening and you'll see the caravan
of excited job seekers ritualistically depositing envelopes in
hopes of securing that perfect job. There are two major problems with this approach. First of all, job seekers should wait at
least seven to ten days before responding to any advertisement
(we'll talk more about that later) and second, by using classi-
fied ads as the sole job source, the job seeker effectively screens
himself out of 80 percent of the available jobs. *Studies show that
less than one out of five jobs are listed in newspapers*. If, for example, your Sunday newspaper has three pages of job listings,
multiply that by five because there are actually fifteen pages of
job openings available—it's just that only three pages of them
are published. It is still tempting to use the Sunday paper as
the primary job source because it is cheap and easy. How else
could a person sit back with a danish and a cup of coffee and
go job hunting? Such a lazy approach is extremely narrow in
scope and drastically reduces your chances of securing employment. This chapter teaches you how to place yourself in the

market for the other twelve pages of job ads that are not in the Sunday paper.

College students, a group of individuals held in protective custody in institutions across America, also have a tendency to use a rather narrow approach to the job market. Instead of reading the Sunday paper, college students truck on down to the placement office to see who's coming to campus. Like the Sunday paper, the campus interview schedule opens up a tiny portion of the job market, representing a minuscule percentage of companies and career opportunities. Most companies do *not* conduct campus visits, and of those that do, relatively few visit any one college. Certainly big-name schools such as Notre Dame and Cal-Tech draw big-name companies to campus, but many of the greatest opportunities of the eighties exist with smaller companies (fifty to one thousand employees) that *never* recruit on campus. Job market exposure is miserable with lesser-known schools, which have difficulty getting companies to visit their campuses and are often forced to rely on local or regional companies to fill the schedule. A small college is not going to attract very many of the Fortune 500 companies.

I don't want to downplay the importance of the Sunday *Chicago Tribune* or your college campus schedule, because each is an effective job search tool. This chapter teaches how to maximize those tools, but more important, it offers many other action avenues that will allow you to tap into the full job market. The job that you secure will affect virtually every aspect of your life, and therefore the job search process warrants a full investigation of career opportunities. *Do your life a favor—take your job search campaign to the street.*

3.2   HOW TO ANSWER JOB ADS

Most job seekers typically read a couple of major Sunday newspapers, scouring the ads for a perfect match against qualifications, and then send out a resume along with a generic cover letter stating how excited they are about the position. That approach is doomed to failure. Finding a job is a numbers game: in a typical job search campaign the job seeker should respond to five to fifteen ads each week Before you say, "Hey, wait a minute, there aren't that many ads that look like a good match!" read on.

Don't limit yourself to a couple of papers such as The Wall Street Journal *and your local paper.* Libraries carry many major newspapers from around the country (often on microfilm); use them for free. If you live in Minneapolis and want to work in Florida, spend a few bucks and subscribe to the Sunday edition of the *Miami Herald* or *Tampa Tribune.* *The National Employment Weekly*, issued by the folks at *The Wall Street Journal*, consolidates all the job ads from each regional edition of the *Journal*. A little effort, Sunday afternoons in the library, and a few dollars and you'll have a nice weekly job ad flow that should *easily* provide many job possibilities each week.

Respond to ads that are up to six months old. Don't laugh. Many jobs are placed on the back burner for months because a new priority came up after the ad was placed, and often it takes six months to fill an opening—especially for middle-management and technical positions. Your resume may land on the desk just when the field has been narrowed to two or three candidates. You could slide right in.

Always wait seven to ten days before responding to any ad. Don't worry about missing an opportunity. You can count on the job selection process to move very slowly. Job ads can generate literally hundreds of responses and you'll increase your chances of success if you give the company time to perform a major weeding out of the candidates before your resume arrives. Remember, most people rush out on Sunday night or Monday to get the resume in the mail and Tuesday through Friday is "glut city" in personnel. Your resume will get much more attention in a stack of ten than in a stack of one hundred. The extra few seconds of review can make the difference between an offer to interview and a form-letter turndown. The only exception to this rule of thumb is when applying for an entry-level, clerical, or production job.

Respond to ads that are one or two levels above the position you are seeking. If a company is advertising for a manager of accounts receivable, there is a likelihood that other vacancies may exist at lower levels in the department. There is often a ripple effect when promotions, transfers, demotions, or reorganizations occur. Job openings often come in sets of two or three. There is also the possibility that even though you aren't qualified for the higher-level job, the company may wish to save money by bringing in a top-notch accounts receivable specialist instead of an expensive manager. *A job ad is much more than a description of a single job opening. A job ad is a solid indicator of activity and change within a company, and specifically within a department.* Answer ads that are above your qualifications to place yourself in the market for hidden jobs.

Respond to ads that are for positions lower than the one you are seeking. A job ad for a personnel clerk simply indicates that a business need exists in a human resources department. Maybe what is really needed is an assistant personnel manager—go for it. Tapping into the hidden job market is the key to job search success.

Never mention salary history or salary required when responding to a job ad. The *only* reason personnel wants to know how much you earn is so that they can screen you out. If the job pays $25,000 per year and you are currently making $15,000, you're screened out. If you are earning $30,000 and the company only wants to pay $25,000, you're screened out. Even if the ad says to include salary history, ignore it. If your qualifications look good, you will still get called in for an interview. If you receive a phone call and are asked about your salary, give a broad range, not a specific amount. In the job search, "He who talks money first—loses."

Job ads are simply indicators that a business need exists. If the ad is for a position in your *general* area of interest, write a nice cover letter highlighting how your background would be specifically valuable. Don't hesitate to respond to ads that are not a perfect match.

3.3   A TWENTY-FOUR HOUR JOB ALERT

There are many indicators in the media and in your daily life that subtly proclaim "job opening here." Put yourself on a twenty-four-hour alert to all job possibilities. The following tips should aim you in the right direction:

1.   Newspaper articles are "job ads" if the article is discussing an expansion program, new plant, personnel change, new product, etc. A company in any state of change is ripe for employment opportunities. Read the newspaper closely and you will be surprised by the number of job leads that you find hidden in various sections. For example, many Sunday papers will announce promotions in the business section. Wait a couple of weeks and write directly to the person who was recently promoted. The first order of business for a newly appointed manager is to build a good staff. Your competition is almost non-existent because the job has not been advertised. The obituary section is sad, and we all feel sympathy for the family of the deceased, but that expired traffic manager has to be replaced. The point I am making is that you should read the newspaper as an investigative job seeker looking for leads.

2.   The ten o'clock news will often carry spots about local businesses. Watch the news with a pencil in hand to note companies that are fighting a union organization attempt or that are breaking ground for a new warehouse. Such news events spell job opportunities.

3.   As you drive around town, look for signs of business change: construction, billboards, new buildings, etc. Changes offer hidden job opportunities. Don't wait for the new Bonanza restaurant to be completed; send a resume to the corporate headquarters in application for night manager or whatever. A new plant or business must have people hired prior to opening.

4. New products on grocery shelves provide a direct link to companies that are growing or diversifying. New products mean new supervisors, new clerks, new marketing analysts, and new salespeople.

Put yourself on a twenty-four-hour job alert for indicators of business change. Transfers, promotions, expansion programs, new products, new buildings, and heavy advertising are all solid indicators of employment opportunities.

3.4 NETWORKING

Networking means using contacts and friends to learn about possible job openings. Forget Uncle Bill's gloom and doom about how the job market is terrible! Forget about your good friend telling you that his company is not hiring! *All companies experience turnover, and regardless of the condition of the company most have probably hired people recently*. Friends and neighbors know that the company is not handing out applications and therefore incorrectly assume that the company is not hiring. Don't worry about job applications. Send a resume to the head of the department that interests you, whether it be maintenance or sales.

Employees quit, die, get fired, have babies, get transferred, get sick, and get promoted every day. New employees must be hired to fill those openings. Some positions are rarely advertised. For example, I worked for a company that hired many people in all levels of human resources yet never once advertised an opening. That company relied on an informal recruiting network and unsolicited resumes from people like you. Your job search strategy should be based on the premise that all companies are hiring at least to cover turnover. Set aside the pessimism of your friends. Putting it nicely, they don't know what the hell they are talking about. Don't ask your relatives and friends whether their companies are handing out applications. (The answer will probably be an emphatic "No!") Ask how their companies are doing in general. Find out if there have been any recent management changes, expansions, or problems. Do the same with all of your contacts:

minister	doctor
dentist	garbage collector
neighbors	relatives
congressperson	religious group
chamber of commerce	Rotary Club
Jaycees	mayor
friends	local business leaders

A visit, for example, to the secretary of the local chamber of commerce can provide many leads about companies moving into the area and other companies that are in a state of change. A phone call to an out-of-town COC could achieve the same. Networking is learning about hidden job opportunities by actively seeking out information from your contacts. Take on the role of an investigator trying to track down companies that may need your services. Be aggressive. Don't ask whether a company is hiring. Ask about business indicators of change. Get that information and you will find job openings.

3.5   INFORMATION INTERVIEWS

An information interview is a way to get an audience with contacts whom you do not personally know but who are in an excellent position to provide job leads. For example, if you are seeking a position in the field of purchasing, you could call up either the V.P. of purchasing or the manager of a local company and request a short meeting to discuss career opportunities in purchasing. Be courteous and up-front about the fact that you are not seeking a job interview, but rather would appreciate his or her career guidance and expertise. Don't ever use an information interview as a format to weasel an interview. Again, make it clear that you just want a few minutes to get some career assistance. Managers are in key positions to know of hidden job opportunities at other companies.

Many job seekers will feel uncomfortable with this method, but it is highly effective for those who are aggressive enough to pursue an information interview. Think about it. In the worst case scenario, the manager may say he is too busy, but in the best case scenario you'll receive valuable job leads and expert advice. Middle managers and V.P.'s are just normal folks who often enjoy helping an individual who is seeking a career in their field.

A valuable by-product of using such a contact is that it enables you to drop a name with another potential employer. Continuing with the previous example, your cover letter or phone call to the company recommended by the purchasing manager should make reference to your discussion with him or her. A name casually mentioned over the phone or in a cover letter is a powerful way to get an interview:

"I met with Mr. Jack Sanders, purchasing manager of Vitron Company, last week and he recommended that a discussion with you regarding a position in your department might be worthwhile. In that regard I have enclosed a resume for your review . . . ."

3.6   JOB ADS IN THE LIBRARY

The public library is hiding literally hundreds of thousands of job opportunities and job openings. Specifically, job openings are spilling out of the reference section. Your librarian is as valuable to you as any job search counselor. To get started in the library, ask for help in finding the following references:

College Placement Annual: The annual is published by the College Placement Council, which is the overseeing formal body of most college placement activities. The council conducts wage surveys and placement research and helps coordinate and develop recruiting and placement standard practices. The *Annual* provides fairly good job search tips, but more important, it lists names and addresses of companies that typically hire college graduates. The annual is organized by discipline and by geographic locations of companies. Use the section that is organized by academic discipline as a guide, but don't be concerned one bit that the company indicates that they are only interested in engineers or M.B.A.'s or B.A.'s in Accounting. That is nonsense. Those companies are probably being controlled by English majors; it's just that it is not cool in our current state of technology hysteria to admit that liberal arts grads are valuable. Also, by screening out certain degrees companies avoid having to deal with the masses—most liberal arts people will accommodate them nicely by simply screening themselves out. NOTE: Companies that typically hire college grads also typically hire clerks, supervisors, typists, and so on. All job seekers can use the *College Placement Annual* as an effective job search tool.

Annual Reports: Annual reports are required to be published by all publicly owned companies. An annual report is simply a brief history of how the company performed in the prior year and what it was up to. Libraries often carry copies of annual reports. You can also phone the personnel department or law department of the company you are interested in and request that they mail one to your home. You should never interview with a publicly owned company without having first read their annual report. The report is a great way to generate questions, and shows the interviewer that you are sincerely interested in the company. Annual reports will let you know about company programs, expansions, and new strategic directions—important job leads.

Take a look at Dun & Bradstreet's *Million Dollar Directory*, Moody's Index, Fortune's *Million Dollar Directory*, and Standard & Poor's Index to develop job leads. Remember that a profitable year for a company will lead the company into a stronger hiring posture. The directories can provide insights to companies that may need you.

Every profession and career field has journals and trade magazines. Your librarian can assist in searching out publications that allow you to tap into the industry. Review three to five trade publications weekly to get job leads via articles, advertisements, and promotion announcements.

Many states publish directories of manufacturing companies. Such directories are fantastic job sources. They often describe the company and list sales volume, products, number of employees, and names and addresses of key officers. You have direct access to virtually every manufacturing company in a given state. If your library doesn't have such a directory, contact the state chamber of commerce for their assistance in borrowing or purchasing a copy.

3.7   STATE JOB SERVICE OFFICE

State job service offices used to be called unemployment offices, but now are heavily geared toward job placement. The job service is much more than a source of minimum-wage jobs; in fact, companies holding government contracts are required to post jobs with the service. Many of the offices have nationwide computer links to help you track down job openings. Don't be embarrassed to visit your local job service office. Certainly a few of them will be staffed with bureaucratic nincompoops, but in many instances, you'll be pleasantly surprised. It's worth a visit to see what they can do to help.

3.8   THE COLLEGE PLACEMENT OFFICE

For college students, the most common mistake in using the college placement office is waiting until the senior year of school. Seniors who meander into the placement office after Christmas break have really missed the boat. Students should get to know the services and people in the placement office no later than freshman year. Placement officials can play an important role in helping land a critically important summer job. They are *paid* to help you in every way possible to land a job. The placement office will often have a library that is a job searcher's dream. Lectures, counseling, videotapes, courses, and more are waiting for you to say, "Help." The placement office should be your base of operations for a job search campaign, not just a place to stop by and sign up for campus interviews. Take full advantage of your placement office! Services include:

Career counseling: Discuss your career plans with expert counselors. They'll advise you to forget IBM if you have a 2.0 G.P.A. and help you get on track with a realistic job search program. They can help you work through philosophical career questions and can help you determine your strengths and liabilities. *See your placement counselor.*

Job search courses: As you'll learn in this book, it takes a lot more than wit, G.P.A., and a nice personality to land a job. Take every course offered by your placement office. Job search is a learned skill, not a natural instinct.

Mock interviews: The opportunity to have a professional criticize your interviewing skills should not be passed by. People in the real world pay thousands of dollars for such help. A simple one-and-a-half day outplacement program can cost thousands of dollars. You can get much more help than that for *free*!

Resource materials: The placement office library is often a goldmine. I'll leave it at that.

The interview schedule: Interview as often as you can within the constraints of the school's rules. If a company does not include your degree on a specification, write a personal letter offering to meet the recruiter at lunch or at his hotel. Show persistence and drive. Don't be so easily screened out by job specs without a fight.

Have I made my point? Use the placement office to your full advantage. Now let me address those who aren't college students, who have been reading this stuff about some kind of placement office. For those job seekers who are not currently in college, wander on over to the college placement office anyway. The schedules and job postings are often on hallway walls that were built with your tax dollars. Check out the wall construction and take good notes. You can't interview on campus, but you can certainly develop a lot of job leads. Write to the recruiters who are coming to campus and request an evening interview. Explain that you are not a college student, but that you are very much interested in interviewing. It is important to note that community colleges will often help you and welcome you to the placement center and let you take full advantage of their services.

3.9   THE JOB SEARCH CAMPAIGN

A haphazard, loosely organized job campaign will work only if luck is injected. Make your own luck by organizing a professional job campaign. Set goals, establish a detailed plan, and keep scrupulous notes of all search activity.

A job seeker who tells me he's mailed out over fifty resumes and still hasn't gotten a positive response gets no sympathy from me. Fifty resumes is nothing! Each campaign must be developed individually, but following is a brief sample of a simple plan. If you are currently employed, reduce the work load appropriately to protect your job, but recognize that reduced effort will mean a longer period of job search.

Weekly Job Search Schedule

1.   Respond to ten job ads.

2.   Complete one information interview.

3.   Send resumes to five companies based on newspaper or trade articles.

4.   Send resumes to five companies selected from the *College Placement Annual*.

5.   Discuss job leads with two contacts. Send one resume as a result.

6.   Send resumes and letters to three companies selected through library research (reference texts).

This campaign will generate about twenty-five letters and resumes per week. Tack into the plan time reserved for research, phone call follow-up, and interviews. *Finding a job is hard work*. Once the letters and resumes get rolling, you will get responses. Expect lots of turndowns. Ninety-nine turndowns and one job offer is a successful campaign. You're just looking for one job.

Pay your dues up front by taking your job search to the street. Plan and organize your effort. Enlist the aid of your friends and relatives to type, keep records, and proofread your material. Get the whole family involved. Finding a job is the most important job you will ever have. Give it everything you've got and you will succeed.

Conclusion

Job opportunities are all around you, not just in the Sunday paper or in the campus interview schedule. Widen your perspective by looking for unpublished or hidden jobs. Remember that 80 percent of all jobs are filled before ever reaching a job ad or interview schedule.

Treat the job search with the respect and priority it deserves. Exhaust all avenues as you aggressively search for a great job. Set aside pessimism and go for it. The jobs are out there on the street. Put down your Sunday paper, finish the danish and coffee, put on your walking shoes, and go after the job you desire. Without a doubt, you can do it.

Before you know it, you'll need to utilize the advice in the next chapter, "How to Prepare for the Interview Better Than Your Competition."

How To Prepare For
The Interview Better
Than Your Competition

4.1 INTRODUCTION

In Olympic gymnastic competition, one hundredth of a point can mean the difference between the glory of gold and the agony of defeat—just *one hundredth of a point*! Long years of preparation, dedication, and hard work are all placed on the line as the gymnast signals "Ready" for the last vault.

As a job seeker, you too have dedicated years of hard work and sacrifices to be qualified for the job market, and when you shake the hand of the interviewer you are signifying "Ready" for your final vault—the interview. Your job search success or failure will rest on your performance in the interview. The comparison with gymnastics splits here because there is no consolation or silver medal for second place in interviewing; just a simple, standard turndown letter. You must strive for the gold by preparing for the interview *better* than your competition. *Those extra hundredths of a point that come with outstanding preparation are often the only difference between an offer and a turndown—and that is a fact.* The decision to present an offer to one candidate rather than another is not nearly as simple or as clear-cut as most job seekers believe. The accomplishments and experiences that you offer are measured against other candidates' equally outstanding accomplishments. Your B.S. degree, grade point average, and work experience are not enough to land a job offer. There will be many candidates interviewed who will have the same or even better resume statistics than yours. You must separate yourself from the competition by those one hundredths of a point to dramatically improve your ratio of offers to interviews. A competitive edge in preparation is critical to your success.

Many of the tasks associated with interview preparation are detail oriented and simple, and may seem rather insignificant or unimportant at first glance, but just as a small backward step after a vault can eliminate the gymnast from competition, a simple bypassed detail of preparation can generate a turndown.

It has always amazed me that so few candidates adequately prepare for interviews. You will gain a powerful competitive edge by learning how to achieve those hundredths of a point via outstanding preparation. *Go for the gold*!

4.2   THE RIGHT ATTITUDE

Your attitude should reflect a professional awareness that an interview is a business meeting between two potential business *partners*. The employer has specific business requirements and you may be the best person to satisfy them. You also have needs and the employer may satisfy them. Don't be ingratiating or subservient; such an attitude will only lead to a turndown. Walk into the interview as someone who can help solve a business problem.

Even though the employment process as a whole is a two-way street, *don't dwell on your needs until you receive an offer*. Plan on spending the valuable interviewing time proving that you meet the prospective employer's requirements. Discussing salary, benefits, relocation policy, or other personal concerns before the offer steals valuable time that should be spent proving that you should *get* the offer. Detailed questions regarding personal concerns are much more appropriately handled *after* the company extends an offer. If after receiving an offer you find that the company does not meet your needs, simply send *them* a turndown letter.

Developing an attitude of professional equality is not quite as easy as it sounds. It is natural to fall prey to the "intimidation syndrome" (most candidates do) because the interviewer does stand between you and something you want. Furthermore, there is a certain power justifiably attributed to someone who can affect your destiny. Also, recruiters control the time, method, and place of meeting, all of which serve to fuel the anxiety that leads to intimidation. It is probably unfair, but even in light of those points listed above, *recruiters demand that you not be intimidated*. A professional positive attitude is required. *An intimidated, nervous job seeker stands out like a sore thumb and will rarely receive an offer*. You must psychologically prepare yourself for the interview to reduce those feelings of intimidation. Spend some time reflecting on the following points to assist your developing the right attitude toward the interview.

Believe in yourself. You do have something of value to offer, whether it be dependability, friendliness, technical skills, or a strong work ethic. If you don't believe in yourself, don't expect an offer. *Lack of confidence is one of the major reasons for turndowns*. Entering the job market with a lack of confidence places you in a vicious circle of receiving turndowns which, in turn, support your negative self-image. Get professional guidance if necessary from your minister, guidance counselor, or placement counselor.

Don't artificially build up the importance of one interview. Statistics say that even if you do get an offer from that company you'll probably change jobs in a few years anyway. There are literally thousands of companies who may need your services (often within commuting distance of your home). Remember the job candidate who only wanted to work for IBM, but settled for an unknown upstart company named Apple. With a good job search plan you will turn up many opportunities. Certainly you must develop company preferences, but don't put all your eggs or apples in one basket. Such an attitude is immature and unrealistic and breeds tension, pressure, and intimidation.

Project an image of yourself in the position for which you will be interviewing. In attitude and spirit *become* that trainee, clerk, researcher, or manager. An actor is trained to project himself in a role so that the audience will believe that he really is a private detective, and similarly you must convince the interviewer that you *are* a buyer or salesman or whatever. Internalize the role by projecting yourself into the position of buyer; don't interview as a liberal arts graduate who is hoping to land the job and become one. Understand that the recruiter is not searching for a young graduate who may have the potential to become a buyer; he is searching for a buyer. To an interviewer, there is a big difference between the two; for a job candidate the difference may seem rather subtle. The point I am making is worth another example for clarification. A career changer, such as a teacher who is seeking to start a new career in industry, must project himself into a new role. The teacher must avoid academic buzzwords and use business buzzwords. He must leave the corduroy suit in the closet and replace it with a business suit. He must talk about implementing a new program that reduces absenteeism by 2 percent (business can relate), not how he chaperones athletic events. He must *become* a businessman who just happens to have experience as a teacher.

An attitude of confidence, business maturity, and a belief in yourself must be in hand the moment the interviewer opens the door and says, "Please come in." Without those "tickets," the job interview is an exercise in futility.

4.3   PERSONAL APPEARANCE: ASK ME IF I REALLY CARE

I wish I could say that you are only required to dress neatly, have your hair combed or brushed, and be clean to present a proper appearance for an interview, but as you already know, I can't truthfully say that appearance is not important. Ours is a society that has taught us to judge a book by its cover, not its content. Fashion, style, and image have permeated every part of our lives. Like it or not, your appearance and dress are perceived as a statement of who you are. Companies, since they comprise individuals, place tremendous importance on image. New company logo designs, for example, are released and publicized with as much fervor as if they were major scientific discoveries. We vote, buy products, attend colleges, and choose spouses based on images. Is it any wonder then that I must devote space in this book to discussing the importance of the color of your socks? Let's both put aside our personal philosophies for a moment and examine how to create a physical image that will help generate job offers.

Your primary goal in dressing for an interview is to feel great about the way you look while projecting an image that matches the requirements of the position and company. A certain amount of poise, confidence, and positive attitude is built into an attractive outfit. Invest in conservatively styled quality clothing in natural fabrics or woven blends. Visit a respected apparel shop: forget the two-for-one sales at your friendly local conglomerate. The quality of fit and fabric from a reputable apparel shop will be an obvious cut above polyester mass-produced clothes. The visual difference between a $9.99 dress shirt and a $20 or $30 shirt is obvious to interviewers. Don't scrimp on clothes. *Some interviewers will decide in the first sixty seconds whether they are interested in you or not (based on personal impression) and will then spend the remainder of the interview validating their snap judgment.* John T. Malloy's book *Dress for Success* is a standard reference text on the impact of appearance and is recommended reading, but good old common-sense decisions about your dress will enhance your chances of receiving an offer. Following are some general guidelines to consider:

Guidelines for Men

Suits
YES: Wear dark blue, gray, muted pin-stripes, or very muted brown or dark plaids. A three-piece classic traditional style should be tailored for excellent fit. A good-quality woven blend of natural fibers looks professional.

NO: Bold plaids, bold pinstripes, contrasting slacks and sport coat, or light colors. Don't buy a size 40 regular off the rack—get alterations for a tailored fit. No handkerchief in the breast pocket.

Shirts

YES: A quality, name-brand white button-down or white classic collar is preferred. Pale blue or pale yellow is acceptable. The collar should fit comfortably and the shirt should be ironed professionally.

NO: Contrasting colored collars, stripes, faddish styles, or cufflinks. A tight collar looks terrible and will be uncomfortable. An inexpensive polyester, tumble-dry, no-iron shirt will look like one.

Ties

YES: Conservative stripes of classic designs that complement your suit. Silk or good-quality blends only.

NO: Bold designs, college logos, etc. No bow ties or clip-ons unless you're interviewing for the newsman position at WKRP in Cincinnati. Don't shop for a good deal; shop for a good tie.

Glasses

YES: Spotless glass and frames.

NO: Tinted glasses of any kind, worn frames, or scratched or smudged glass.

Socks

YES: Calf-length, matching or complementing the suit.

NO: Short socks that might expose a hairy leg.

Shoes

YES: Highly polished slip-ons or laced dress shoes; brown, cordovan, or black.

NO: Wing-tipped clunkers, loafers, crepe soles, or faddish styles or colors (gray, blue, etc.).

Watch

YES: Conservative simple watch.

NO: Deep-sea, calculator, or stylishly distracting watch.

(Special note for Purdue engineering grads: Leave your electronic game watches in the dorm.)

Hair

YES: Traditional short business cut is preferred, but a medium-length cut (slightly over the ears) is acceptable.

NO: Faddish cuts or hair that is more than halfway over the ears will not work to your advantage. (High school and college grads take note.)

Guidelines for Women

Suits, Dresses

YES: Conservative business suit or dress of natural or woven-blend fabric; always below knee-length. Ask a businesswoman friend to recommend a respected apparel shop. Choose a soft color that complements your skin tone and hair color; brown, tan, beige, blue, or gray.

NO: Bold colors or dramatic prints are out. The style shouldn't disguise the fact that you are a woman, but it shouldn't overpower the recruiter with a statement of femininity either. Don't look manly yet don't look like a dinner date.

Blouses

YES: Simple style; white or soft colors.

NO: Low-cut necklines or high-necked ruffles.

Shoes

YES: Highly polished pumps or medium heels in a color that matches your outfit.

NO: Three-inch heels or docksiders.

Stockings

YES: Beige, tan, or natural.

NO: Textures or faddish colors.

Purse

YES: Medium or small size in a color that goes with your outfit.

NO: Large bag bulging with "stuff."

Hair

YES: A hair style that does not distract from your goal to achieve an image of professional maturity.

NO: Any hair style that is distracting because it does not flatter your facial structure or age, or that is faddishly stylish.

Nails, Jewelry, Perfume, and Makeup

YES: Clear or lightly tinted nail polish, minimal jewelry, understated natural makeup.

NO: Brightly colored nail polish, large earrings, or more than two finger rings. Very light perfume is acceptable, but why risk offending?

Summary

Just in case you haven't noticed, the preceding dress guidelines for men and women are ridiculous. Does it really matter what color your socks or stockings are? Will your large hoop earrings negatively affect your potential performance as a management trainee? Does the color or style of your suit affect your leadership skills? No, no, and no. Many job candidates recognize the absurdity of the guidelines and arrive at the interview dressed as "themselves" carrying an attitude of, "Hey, if you don't want to hire me as I am then I don't want to work for you!" *The interview is not the time to make a personal statement of nonconformity or disagreement with society's concept of professional image.* It is against both federal and moral laws to discriminate based on appearance, but I ask you, how many bankers have full beards? How many professional salesmen are sloppy and poorly groomed? How many female computer company representatives wear heavy, high-fashion makeup? Image is important to all companies.

The guidelines listed in this chapter will serve you well in almost all interviewing situations. Generally speaking, you can't overdress for an interview. It is a compliment to any company that you bothered to dress professionally for the interview. High fashion and trendy dress are sometimes appropriate for certain positions in the entertainment or fashion industry, but the classic professional look is the rule of thumb. You are a product; package it well to sell in the job market.

4.4 RESEARCHING THE COMPANY: A WORTHWHILE INVESTMENT OF TIME

Most candidates prepare for the interview by *maybe* skimming the annual report or (if a college student) the standard reference materials in the placement center. Such preparation is the absolute minimum that entitles you to sit down for the interview. Shallow research preparation will provide only basic data: facility locations, product lines, and possibly a brief sketch of career programs. Big deal! Every candidate knows at least that much. It doesn't impress an interviewer one bit that you know that Ameri-Can Company has a plant in Denver or that they have a three-phase training program. Most candidates know basic facts about the company and most candidates get turndowns. By going one step beyond the standard research effort you can dramatically separate yourself from the competition and at the same time go one step up on the evaluation rating. The following activities will get you pointed in the direction of a job offer:

Learn the name(s), pronunciations, and titles of your interviewers in advance. Simply ask the person who extended the invitation.

Recruiter: "John, this is Mr. Callio of our Research Department."
John Candidate: "Pleased to meet you sir. *I understand that you are manager of the plastics division.*"

(Mr. Callio is impressed that you know his position and that you have the assertiveness to initiate the discussion. He can now begin discussing his needs.)

Study the annual report and memorize key facts that reflect the company's direction, recent changes in organization, and strategic plans.

Recruiter: "John, it wasn't listed on the job description, but the opening we have is located at our facility in Tulsa."

John Candidate: "According to your annual report, the Tulsa plant has recently been enhanced by a three-million-dollar modernization project. Did that project generate a new requirement for an industrial analyst?"

(The recruiter now knows that you prepared beyond the standard effort. He is impressed with your knowledge and believes that you really are interested in his company. The conversation will now naturally flow to his specific needs in Tulsa.)

Get inside information about the company and plan to use it in the interview. Request literature on new products from a sales office, call up the public affairs or law department and request general informational pamphlets, or even call a specific department and ask to speak to someone in your field (engineer, trainee, etc.) to discuss career paths. Contact a relative or friend of a friend who works at the company.

Recruiter: "Our sales program is a three-month controlled tour in all product lines."
John Candidate: "Your brochure described the program enough to really pique my interest. I talked with Sarah Smith, a salesperson in your Indianapolis office, and she discussed how the phased tour really formed a solid educational foundation for a career in sales. The tour sounds like an excellent mix of classroom and on-the-job training."

(John Candidate has proved enthusiasm, innovativeness, and assertiveness—all attributes of a salesperson. Also, John Candidate has indicated that he knows someone in the company; he is now an "insider.")

Research the library for articles about the company that have appeared in trade magazines, weekly periodicals, or business newspapers, etc. Get inside information to use in the interview.

Recruiter: "John, our company is on a track to double revenues in three years, and we need strong, creative leadership to get us there."
John Candidate: "Yes, I was pleased to read an article in a December issue of *Business Week* that praised your employee in-

volvement program and discussed how the resulting productivity improvements have really bolstered the future outlook. I agree that the challenges you offer require a strong participative leader. I have a proven track record in participative management. Last year . . . ."

(John Candidate has proved interest, sincerity, and a sharp recall ability. Furthermore, he has smoothly set himself up to prove his leadership ability.)

Contact the local chamber of commerce for general information on taxes, housing, climate, etc.

Recruiter: "John, I think you'd find that living in the Chicago area offers many cultural and educational advantages."
John Candidate: "Prior to the interview I requested some information from the chamber of commerce and I agree 100 percent. The annual festival on Navy Pier sounds fantastic and I never realized the city offered so much diversity of cultural attractions. The lakefront is beautiful. Now, if it just didn't snow so much."

(John Candidate has proved interest, sincerity, and a sense of humor.)

The decision to make an offer or send a turndown hinges on nuances that separate you from an equally qualified competitor. Do not make the mistake of downplaying the importance of preparatory research. It is always obvious to recruiters how much effort has gone into your preparation, and the degree of preparation is viewed as a barometer of your drive, ambition, creativity, interest, and enthusiasm. Thorough research preparation will really pay off.

4.5 VOCATIONAL MATURITY

Vocational maturity is having clearly defined goals, realistic expectations, and a specific idea of how you can contribute to a company's profitability. *It is your job to know what you can do and what you want.* Don't ever ask for guidance or counseling from a recruiter. It is not a part of the recruiter's job to figure out a career path that would best suit your needs. Attaining vocational maturity is an especially difficult task for young graduates who may never have even worked in their academic disciplines. If you are an engineer, for example, who has worked as a waitress for the past four summers, seek guidance to assist in determining whether you would like field engineering or research and development, but don't ask the recruiter. If you have a degree in business administration there are myriad career paths available; don't ask an interviewer to pick one for you. Vocational maturity requires defining goals, conducting a self-analysis of skills, weaknesses, likes and dislikes, and developing an understanding of how certain industries and positions within those industries might mesh with your defined needs. Many candidates think that it is the recruiter's job to figure all that out in a thirty-to-forty-five minute interview. *No way!* A recruiter cannot function as your vocational guidance counselor.

There is at least a ton of books written by counselors and psychologists on the topic of figuring out your life and what you want to do with it and there are many avenues of action ranging from informational interviews to facility tours that can help. Your best bet is to go to the library and review the materials written by career-planning expert Richard N. Bolles and/ or see a counselor. Bolles offers many excellent self-evaluatory tools and much solid advice on how to determine career paths that will lead you to self-fulfillment. *Just don't ask the interviewer.*

The Bottom Line on Reimbursement of Interview Expenses

Many candidates are apprehensive about interview expenses. There you are having completed a great interview in which you discussed your future and the fantastic opportunities at Ajax Corporation when you realize that you must change the subject and ask for your money back for the Holiday Inn room and dinner at Sumiaki's Oyster House. Somehow it seems ridiculously incongruous. There are enough challenges in the job search process without having to worry about expenses. Let's look at the issue of reimbursement from the company's perspective.

It is standard practice to reimburse interviewees for *all normal* expenses incurred if the interview requires your traveling more than thirty miles to another city or state. If the interview site is within thirty miles of your home, don't ask for or expect reimbursement, even though on occasion the company may offer to pick up parking and mileage expenses. Asking for ten dollars for mileage or lunch doesn't reflect well on your business maturity or interest. Companies expect to pay for interview expenses, and reimbursement is viewed as simple business etiquette; no more, no less. Companies already know that the hotel is expensive and that the rental car costs $40 a day plus mileage. Don't worry about it. Companies do vary on reimbursement procedures, though, so it is to your advantage to ask certain questions at the time of the invitation to interview:

1. "Mr. Veith, how will the reimbursement for expenses be handled?"

2. "Will I be reimbursed through the mail after the interview or will it be handled the same day?"

3. "Is there a fixed per diem rate (daily) for meals and lodging?"

4. "Do you recommend a particular hotel?"

Find out the company's procedures. It is not a hush-hush sensitive topic. Reimbursement is a normal business cost. I said earlier that companies reimburse for all *normal* expenses. (Following is a detailed explanation of "normal.")

Normal reimbursable expenses: Lodging, food, and travel to get you there and back in the most common-sense manner.

1. Mid-size or compact rental car. Don't rent a sports car or luxury car (you think I'm kidding?). Also, if you don't carry a major credit card, be sure to call the rental agency to see if they require a heavy cash deposit.

2. Tolls, parking, and tips to porters and waiters are legitimate expenses.

3. Reserve coach airfare, not first class. Don't use the interview as a layover on your way to visit a friend. The full route shown on the receipt will raise doubt as to the sincerity of your interest.

4. All car mileage associated with getting there and back is legitimate. This includes mileage to the airport, etc. Twenty-one cents per mile is the standard reimbursed rate.

5. Reasonable meals. Taking advantage of the company will cloud your integrity. Six dollars for breakfast, eight dollars for lunch, and sixteen dollars for dinner (total $30 per day) will generally not raise eyebrows. Food costs do vary from region to region; always order a medium-priced entree on the menu. Ask the company to reimburse you for a good meal, not a culinary experience. Always have your receipts available.

6. Lodging. Usually a reservation will be made for you by the company, but if the decision is yours, choose a *standard* name-brand hotel.

7. Don't ask to be reimbursed for alcoholic beverages, entertainment, toiletries, or more than one phone call per day.

8. It is not normal procedure with most companies to send prepaid airline tickets or to send money to you prior to the interview. Don't ask for such a favor.

The bottom line on interviewing expenses is that you should ask about the procedures prior to the interview and be honest, fair, and ethical in presenting your claim.

Conclusion

Most job candidates extend minimal effort in preparation for an interview, and weak preparation is always obvious. You will realize a tremendous competitive edge in the selection process by separating yourself from the competition with outstanding preparation. It is those tiny nuances of excellent presentation that often make the difference between offer and turndown. The interview is your final vault. Go for a perfect 10.

Interview Preparation Checklist

Positive, confident attitude
Project yourself into the
    position
Clearly defined goals
Company research
Studied annual report and
    literature
Names, titles of
    interviewers
Have inside information

Appearance (Men)

Quality suit
Expertly ironed shirt
Good collar fit
Spotless glasses

Calf-length socks
Highly polished shoes
Conservative watch
Medium to short haircut

Appearance (Women)

Quality suit or dress, below
    knee-length, simple style
Spotless glasses
Small/medium-size purse
Clear or lightly tinted nail
    polish
Minimal jewelry
Understated makeup
Beige, tan, or natural
    stockings

The Job Interview

5.1 INTRODUCTION

A job interview is a business meeting between a job candidate and one or more interviewers. The purpose is to determine whether a match exists between what the company requires and what the candidate offers. The process is usually completed in a formal setting such as a business office or campus interviewing room, but may also take place in a hotel room or restaurant, or even on a golf course. The length of a job interview ranges from about twenty minutes to a two-day facility visit. It is important to understand the format and structure of job interviews to avoid surprises and to reduce any anxiety that results from fear of the unknown. Knowing what to expect will increase interviewing effectiveness and generate more offers. This chapter presents a detailed analysis of the two major types of job interviews: (1) the preliminary or screening interview and (2) the selection interview.

5.2 THE PRELIMINARY OR SCREENING INTERVIEW

The preliminary or screening interview occurs when a phone call, resume, letter, or application has piqued the company's interest enough for them to believe that a possible match exists or, in the case of college placement, when a student simply signs up on the interview schedule. At this stage in the employment selection process, the company knows very little or perhaps nothing about the candidate! In college campus recruitment, for example, companies often know *only* that the candidates on the interview schedule have certain specified degree(s). Many candidates are granted preliminary interviews and all but a handful are screened out. In a typical recruiting year at one major university, 25,000 preliminary interviews are scheduled for 850 employers. The offer ratio to receive an invitation for a selection interview ranges from 10 to 50 percent. This means that a typical Fortune 500 company may send turndowns to 90 percent of those initially interviewed. *The purpose of a preliminary interview is to perform a gross weeding-out of candidates. Your only goal in a preliminary interview is to avoid being screened out.* This implies that you will not ask questions about benefits or what it's like living in Butte, Montana, but will *direct your entire focus toward proving that you meet the company's requirements.*

Preliminary interviews usually come in a nice tidy package; a standard format. A preliminary interview with a small electronics company in Tampa, Florida, for example, will be structured just like an initial interview taken on the campus of the University of Michigan. To learn what to expect in a preliminary interview, we'll examine the standard format and discuss each section:

Standard Preliminary or Screening Interview Format

Step I: The Warm-up   **4 minutes**
    —Greeting
    —Establish Rapport
    —Explain Structure of Interview
    —Verify Data on Resume, etc.

Step II: Gather Evaluation Data   **15 minutes**
    —Open-ended Questions
    —Probing Questions

—Closed Questions
—Determine whether Match Exists
—Strengths, Liabilities

Step III: Answer Questions/Offer Information   8 minutes
—Explain Training Program
—Describe Position
—Answer Candidate's Questions

Step IV: Close Interview   3 minutes
—Explain What Happens Next
—Hand Out Company Brochure

Total: 30 minutes

Most clearheaded people would agree that it just doesn't seem fair that the career fate of a job candidate hinges on such a brief format, which provides, at best, a cursory review of qualifications and strengths. Interviewing is a process of educated guesswork and is not always fair. Without a doubt, many candidates who receive turndowns surely could have been just as successful in the position as the candidate who received the offer. There's no use complaining, though, because the standard format is the only game in town. Your only recourse in the job search is to channel your energies to perform better than the competition. To assist in that direction, let's take a close look at each step of the preliminary interview.

Step I: The Warm-up

In Step I the recruiter is formulating a critical first impression. Absolutely required on your part is a firm handshake, a smile, and an initiating statement that immediately sets a positive tone for the interview. It is not your job to seek control of the interview, but you must exude confidence, poise, assertiveness, and enthusiasm during the first few minutes. Maintain an excellent posture, choose a chair that is located close to the interviewer and don't fidget or act nervous. With excellent preparation in hand, your demeanor should be beaming with an obviously high energy level; you're *ready*! Following are some example initiating statements:

Initiating Statement: "Good morning Mr. Harvey. I'm pleased to meet you. After receiving your invitation to interview last week, I requested a copy of your annual report and am now even more excited about the opportunities with AmeriCan Corporation. I was particularly impressed with the success of your new product line of two-piece cans. The 20 percent market share must have really pleased the stockholders. Are you doing as well this quarter?"
Comment: The candidate has shown assertiveness and confidence and has recognized the importance of the stockholders and the bottom line. He has also complimented the company on the success of their new product. The interview is off to a good start.

Initiating Statement: "Good afternoon, Mrs. Laughton. After all of the discussions we have had on the phone, I have been looking forward to meeting you in person. This new office complex is quite a structure. I understand that the corporate departments have just moved in from the old facility on Tenth Avenue. Are you pleased with the move?"
Comment: The candidate has exhibited enthusiasm, assertiveness, and excitement for the interview. He has also scored well on interest and preparation by having learned about the office move prior to the interview.

Initiating Statement (campus interview): "Good morning, Mr. Ackerman. Welcome to the snow capital of the Midwest. If you haven't been outside lately, I've got to tell you that there is a blizzard going on. I just walked over from my dorm and it is freezing. Do you get much snow in Charleston?"
Comment: The candidate has shown assertiveness, confidence, and an outgoing friendliness. Solid interest and interview preparation are already implied by the candidate's awareness that Mr. Ackerman is based in Charleston. All of this was accomplished in twenty seconds!

Initiating Statement: "Hello, Mr. O'Kelliher. How are you

today? By the way, I must compliment you on your efficient and courteous staff. I arrived about ten minutes early and Stephanie gave me an application, some informational brochures, and a cup of coffee. She seems like a very nice woman."

Comment: The candidate has initiated the interview with confidence, poise, sensitivity, and assertiveness. A pleasant and friendly first impression.

The first minute is absolutely critical to interviewing success. Many interviewers will make a snap judgment about you— good or bad—and spend the remainder of the time validating the first impression. Certainly some job seekers are going to be uncomfortable initiating an interview as described in the previous examples. Most job candidates walk into the office, shake a hand and then meekly sit down to await the first question. That makes for a very poor first impression. You certainly shouldn't be artificially assertive or offer a feigned compliment, but armed with the attitude that the interview is a business meeting between two equals, you should simply take the initiative in your own personal style. *Exhibit confidence, enthusiasm and a high level of interest in the first minute of the interview. Be yourself and do it your own way, but do it!*

Step II: Gather Evaluation Data

Step II is the real meat of the interview. The interviewer knows which strengths and qualifications he is seeking and in this part of the interview will ask questions to support the overall evaluation. There are seven general evaluatory categories (discussed in detail in Chapter Nine):

1. Personal impression

2. Communication skills

3. Enthusiasm

4. Leadership

5. Competence

6. Vocational maturity

7. Interest

To gather evaluation data, three types of questions will be used: **open-ended**, **probing**, and **closed**. Job candidates must recognize the purpose and type of question being asked to determine the appropriate response.

Open-Ended Questions

An open-ended question is an interviewer's fishing trip to try to catch evaluatory information. Such questions are broad in scope and afford the candidate tremendous flexibility in response. Outstanding preparation is the key to handling open-ended questions. Assuming that the candidate knows which strengths are required for the position, he can use the broad parameter of an open-ended question to prove one or more prerequisite strengths:

Open-ended question: "What is your management style?" (for the purpose of this example, assume that the company is an innovative, high-tech growth company. Prior to the interview the candidate has developed a list of strengths that are important for this position and will use this question to prove that he has a management style that meshes with the firm's policy.)

Candidate's Response: "I am a strong advocate of developing an entrepreneurial climate and my management style is one of establishing strategic goals and direction and providing the encouragement and freedom to my team to get us there as quickly as possible. My job as a manager is to get the herd heading roughly west, not to prescribe a narrow trail. I have found that unleashed creativity, enthusiasm, and innovative resourcefulness get results. For example . . ."

Open-ended question: "Tell me about yourself." (Assume that the candidate has researched well and knows that strong communication skills are required to land this position.)

Candidate's Response: "I'm glad you asked that question, because although my resume and application have outlined basic facts regarding my accomplishments, they haven't touched on what I feel is one of my greatest strengths—the ability to communicate effectively with all levels of management. Through my experience, I have increasingly recognized the importance of communications and, in particular, how effective communications can play a key role in achieving results. For example, last fall . . ."

Comment: Many candidates would have answered this question by rambling on about extracurricular activities in high school or college, hobbies, family life, or other interesting but relatively unimportant information. Instead, this candidate seized the question as an opportunity to prove a strength that he knows is required to land the job.

Open-ended question: "Why should I hire you?" (In this example, assume that the candidate is interviewing for a management trainee position in insurance sales that requires a high degree of self-motivation and persistence.)

Candidate's Response: "I believe you should hire me because my record of performance and achievements is a strong indicator that I will be successful in sales and will contribute to your company's profitability. In insurance sales you need a highly motivated self-starter who has the persistence and drive to go for that one more sales call late on a Friday afternoon. I am that kind of person. I have always been extremely competitive and persistent in reaching established goals. For example . . ." (candidate now uses examples to prove self-motivation and persistence).

Open-ended questions provide a real opportunity for a candidate to prove that he or she meets the requirements of the position. Many candidates respond to open-ended questions by offering meandering, nondirected statements that could best be termed "interview gobbledygook." Thorough interview preparation and a good understanding of the strengths required to land the job are the keys to success in answering open-ended questions. A good response to an open-ended question clearly and logically provides valuable positive information to support an outstanding rating in one of the seven evaluation categories.

Common Open-ended Questions

1. Discuss two or three factors that are most important to you in a job.

2. Describe your ideal job.

3. What are your short-term goals?

4. What are your long-term goals?

5. What is your greatest strength?

6. What is your greatest weakness?

7. In your opinion, what is success?

8. What is your greatest accomplishment?

9. Do you consider yourself a good manager?

10. How are you better than the other candidates I interviewed today?

11. What interests you most about this job?

12. What have you learned from your failures or mistakes?

13. What have you learned from your college experience?

14. What were your favorite subjects? Why?

15. What were your least favorite subjects? Why?

16. Tell me about your work experience.

17. How can you contribute to our company?

18. Why do you feel you have management potential?

19. How do you feel about your academic background?

20. What motivates you?

21. What is the biggest mistake you ever made?

Probing Questions

A probing question implies that the interviewer is not yet convinced, is not completely satisfied with a particular response, or is exploring a new area of concern. He may be seeking additional information to validate a strength or liability. A probing question is usually direct and to the point. The job seeker's task is to determine if a strength or liability is being questioned and handle the response appropriately.

Probing Question: "Why are you interested in working for our company?" (The recruiter is seeking to gauge the candidate's level of interest and perhaps his vocational maturity.)

Candidate's Response: "I have placed significant importance on researching potential companies and there are a number of reasons why I am especially interested in Ameri-Can Corporation. I called up your sales office in Minneapolis to request some general information and your regional manager, Mr. Grow, provided an extensive review of your training program. I was particularly excited to learn that . . ."

Probing Question: "Were you ever involved in any leadership activities?" (The interviewer is seeking information to evaluate leadership potential. The response to this question will determine the leadership rating.)

Candidate's Response: "I have taken on leadership roles in many areas of my college life, from social clubs to athletics. For example . . ." (candidate uses an example from his background to prove leadership potential).

Probing Question: "Why did you choose to major in history?" (The interviewer knows that the degree in history is not directly applicable to the job and, in fact, views the degree as a *liability*. The interviewer is giving the candidate a shot to prove that he is the best choice in spite of the history degree.)

Candidate's Response: "Studying history is really learning the business of man: motivations, mistakes, logic, and development. I have always been fascinated with reviewing historical data and plugging it into today's social environment. My major is a legitimate concern because it has not offered a specialized skill. I understand that the position of management trainee in human resources systems requires solid communication skills and an ability to assimilate data to support a wide variety of business activities ranging from management development to manpower planning. My greatest strengths are communications and analysis. Last summer . . ."

Probing Question: "How would you rate your last boss?" (The recruiter is checking out the "attitude" and professional maturity of the candidate. *Negative remarks about a prior company or boss will always spell turndown.*)

Candidate's Response: "I have worked for a number of supervisors in the last few years and have learned and profited from each one. I think my own management style comprises a little bit of each of my former mentors. My most recent boss was an open, participative manager who was an expert in delegation. We were responsible for one project that . . ." (candidate presents an example to prove delegation or managerial skill.)

Probing questions don't provide quite as much flexibility of response as open-ended questions, but will often point directly to an interviewer's concern regarding a strength or a liability. *Relax in the interview and listen to the question before responding.* Focus your response on proving that you have the required strengths or on neutralizing the interviewer's concern about a liability.

Common Probing Questions

1. Are you open for relocation?

2. Why did you decide to attend this college?

3. How would you evaluate your last boss?

4. What didn't you like about your previous employer?

5. Why have you been unemployed for so long?

6. Do you consider yourself a creative person?

7. What other companies are you considering?

8. Why didn't you get better grades in school?

9. What makes you think that you can effectively supervise?

10. Why are you interested in this position?

11. Do you work independently?

12. Why are you seeking a career change?

13. What is your geographic preference?

14. To what extend have you been involved in extracurricular activities?

15. Do you have any hobbies or special interests?

16. Are you in good health?

17. Have you had any courses in _____ ?

18. How do you handle yourself under stressful situations?

19. Why do you want to leave your employer after only two years?

20. How would you describe your study habits?

Closed Questions

Closed questions are easy money. The interviewer must validate basic factual data and will ask short closed questions to fill in the blanks on the interviewing form. The interviewer is obviously not interested in a great dissertation from the job candidate. He wants to get his data quickly and move on to more important open-ended and probing questions. Your task at hand is to answer the questions in a conversational manner that will prevent the interview from turning into an interrogation format.

Closed Question: "What is your phone number?"

Candidate's Response: "My home phone number is 214-996-1800. [pause while the recruiter is writing] I can also be reached at my office, 214-844-2578."

Comment: Don't answer closed questions like a robot. It is tempting to just feed back the numbers. In this example the candidate paused as the recruiter wrote—a simple, courteous response.

Closed Question: "When will you be available for employment?"

Candidate's Response: "I have an excellent relationship with my employer and would appreciate the flexibility to allow two weeks' notice. This would allow ample time to get things in order to ease the transition of my replacement. Is that an acceptable time frame to meet your requirements?"

Comment: The candidate could have simply said, "Two weeks," a curt abbreviated reply that leads the interviewer to a dead end. Instead, this candidate subtly offered a couple of positive nuances including his excellent working relationship with his employer and a professional concern to ease the transition of his replacement. He ended with a question that served to keep the interview flowing in a conversational manner.

Closed Question: "Would you mind sending me an official copy of your transcripts?"

Candidate's Response: "No problem. In fact, in anticipation of your request I have an unofficial transcript with me. Our school is not known for its expediency in sending transcripts so this may be useful in the interim while you are waiting to receive an official copy from the registrar."

Comment: Talk about being prepared! This candidate knew that his school was slow in sending transcripts and went to the trouble of having one on hand for the recruiter. The interviewer can only be impressed.

Closed questions present little threat or difficulty to a job candidate. Usually the interviewer is simply seeking factual data, e.g. home address. To keep the interview flowing, *reply to closed questions in a conversational manner whenever possible*. While he is writing down your address, mention that you recently organized a block party, etc. Offer comments that will keep the interview moving and will help the interviewer go on to another question. An interview must flow like a pleasant conversation, not like a third-degree inquisition. You have to help.

Summary

Listen carefully to all questions and don't rush your responses. Constantly direct and focus attention on those
strengths required to receive the job offer. Practice answering
the common questions I have listed. The fifteen-minute period
of Step II is the most important part of the interview. (Chapters 6 and 7 are dedicated entirely to teaching how to handle
liabilities and how to prove strengths.)

Step III: Answer Questions/Offer Information

In Step III of the standard format, the recruiter will solicit
questions and offer general and specific information about the
job and the company. It is *expected* that you will have some
questions. Telling the recruiter that he's done such a fine job
that you don't have any questions is grounds for a turndown.
Such a statement implies the ridiculous assumption that in fifteen minutes you have received all of the information you need
regarding this career opportunity. Be prepared for each interview by having at least two or three questions in your back
pocket that could be utilized during this part of the interview.
The questions should zero in on the company's requirements:

1. Is this vacancy the result of a promotion?

2. What are the major responsibilities of this position?

3. What qualities are you seeking in the person to fill this
    job?

4. What authority would I have as a _____ ?

5. Where would I fit in on the organizational chart?

6. What are the major strengths of Ameri-Can Corpora-
    tion?

7. Who are your major competitors?

8. What are the major priorities of this position?

9. Whom would I report to?

10. What happened to the last person who held this job?

As the interviewer answers your questions and offers information about the company and the position, be prepared to prove (Chapter 6) that you have key strengths that are brought up. For example, if you haven't yet proved your interest, now might be the time. *Maintain your excitement and enthusiasm throughout the interview.*

Step IV: Close Interview

The interviewer will close by explaining the notification procedure. It is important for you to know how the next contact will be made—phone, letter, telegram, etc.—and how long it will take to make the decision. The recruiter will probably give the shortest possible time frame. Expect to wait longer.

As you leave the interview, again exhibit poise, assertiveness, enthusiasm, confidence, and interest. Don't just say thank you and then meekly exit.

Exit Statement: "Thank you very much for your time. The rotating assignment of your training program has me even more excited about the position. I feel confident that I can contribute to Ameri-Can Corporation and will be looking forward to your letter. Have a good day, Mr. Miller."

Comment: The candidate has reaffirmed his interest and belief that he can contribute to the company and by using the interviewer's name has closed on a personal note.

Exit Statement: "Thank you very much for this opportunity, Mr. Callio. The unique challenge offered in sales is the best I've seen. I am very much interested and believe that I can contribute to Ameri-Can's profit. I'll be looking forward to your decision. Have a good day, sir."

Exit Statement: "Thank you very much for the hospitality. I have enjoyed our meeting and am convinced that my background and track record will facilitate my immediately contributing to Ameri-Can. Thanks again, Mr. Meister. If you should require any additional information, please feel free to call at my office. Have a nice day and a safe trip back home."

Presenting an exit statement only makes common sense— right? Hundreds of candidates that I have interviewed meekly offer a thank-you and then quickly disappear out the door. Don't make that mistake. As a final note on exits, be sure to thank the secretary or receptionist who ushered you in to the interviewer—*by name. End the interview with the same high-energy professional impression that you made in the first minute.*

5.3   THE SELECTION INTERVIEW

The selection interview is the final step leading to an offer. If the candidate has survived the preliminary interview cut, he proceeds to a more in-depth interview format. The competition for the job has now been dramatically narrowed to a few candidates. An interesting note for college students to consider is that if a company is extremely picky in the preliminary interviewing process and weeds out, for example, 90 percent of those initially interviewed, then the offer ratio in the selection interview stage will probably be very high. In that scenario, the company has been very selective, has decided that they are very much interested in you and are using the selection interview as a final "look-see" and recruiting tool. The focus has shifted to recruit *you*. On the other hand, if a company offers selection interviews (facility visits) to 50 percent of those initially interviewed, the offer ratio in the selection interview will be low. At the very least, you should be pleased that you made the first cut. Selection interviews will vary in structure ranging from a two-hour dinner interview to a two-day facility visit. Following are descriptions of what to expect and tips on succeeding in the selection interview.

The Dinner Interview
The dinner or luncheon interview will usually take place in a fairly nice restaurant that offers a quiet atmosphere. Plan to arrive twenty minutes early to allow a "freshening-up" visit to the restroom. A crooked tie, a belt that is not centered, mussed hair, or an open fly is disastrous. You also need a few minutes to relax before meeting the interviewer(s).

The dinner interview should be a much softer sell than the preliminary interview (where you went for the jugular to prove that you meet the requirements). The company feels reasonably assured that you can do the job, but now needs to confirm that you fit in with the company. Your personal demeanor will be a primary factor in this type of interview. Let the interviewer guide the topics of discussion, but occasionally reinforce an important prerequisite strength. Don't be surprised to find conversation oriented toward politics, movies, or other general issues unrelated to the job. The interviewer is interested in knowing about you as a human being. Avoid taking a controversial stand on any issue, e.g., "For my money, Jerry Falwell is our best bet for President."

It may be tempting to get overly familiar with the interviewer after you share a few laughs and start hitting it off. Don't let your guard down. *Maintain a professional attitude*. This is still a business meeting.

Order a light entree that is easy to eat. *You* should be the center of attention, not the plateful of steamed Maryland crabs. *Never order alcoholic beverages*. Forget the glass of wine with dinner or a cocktail at the bar. Order a glass of Perrier water, soda with a twist of lime, iced tea, or coffee. The recruiter can only respect your professionalism in wishing to maintain a clear head for this important business meeting.

Use excellent manners. Candidates who don't dine often in fine restaurants should review a basic etiquette book. Tucking a dinner napkin down one's pants is just not acceptable.

Even if the interviewer invites you to have a smoke—don't! Do not smoke under any circumstances. Maintain a professional image. If you are a non-smoker, don't make a fuss if the interviewer lights up. Accommodate his or her habit. Put up your NO SMOKING sign *after* you get the job. The key to succeeding in a dinner or luncheon interview is to relax and present yourself as a well-rounded, intelligent, and nice person.

The Secondary Interview/Facility Visit

The facility visit (plant trip) is usually a formalized, heavily structured set of activities lasting for one or two days. The company must be very interested in you because the cost of your travel and the time commitment of company personnel is very costly. A soft sell is all that will be necessary to land the job. "Do we like this candidate?" will be the primary factor of the final decision. Be friendly, assertive, confident, and poised. Be nice. I know this doesn't sound corporate, but the final decision often comes down to a feeling of "Would I like to have this person as a next-door neighbor?" The company knows you can do the job; the question is "Do you fit in?"

Typical Agenda: Facility Visit

1. **Breakfast Meeting With Host.**   This is a welcome meeting to explain the overall agenda, to learn whom you'll be meeting, and perhaps to gather the expense receipts so a cash reimbursement can be provided at the end of the day. Request the names and titles of those you will be meeting and write them down on a notepad. People feel good when they are recognized. Be prepared with *specific* questions about the company and the job. At this stage, the focus is shifting to *your* needs and *your* interests. This company is recruiting you. Enjoy it, but *never act egotistical*. You haven't received the offer yet! *Being egotistical will always generate a turndown*.

2. **Brief Interview With High-Level Manager.**   This is another welcome session, but this time by the person who authorizes the offer letter. The top brass likes to show interest in new hires, and it is proper business etiquette for a high-level manager to welcome candidates to the facility. You'll receive a brief hello, some small talk, and a cup of coffee. You'll probably see this person again at the end of the interviewing day.

3. **Facility Tour.**   You can expect a fairly extensive tour of the facility or departments. The tour is designed to answer your specific questions about the company and the job. Take note of new equipment or areas of which the host is particularly proud. You'll want to mention them later in the day when you meet the high-level manager again. Show outward signs of interest and enthusiasm.

The company is probably extremely proud that they have the biggest twine-ball rolling machine in the Western hemisphere. Share their excitement.

4. **Luncheon.** Companies will often arrange a luncheon with your peers to provide an opportunity for you to ask them questions about employment with the company. Be aware that they may be required to submit an evaluation of your potential. *Maintain professionalism*.

5. **Afternoon Meeting With Supervisors.** You may meet with two or three supervisors individually or as a group to let them look at you. Your qualifications are not in question; your personality and attitude are. Be friendly and outgoing and come across as a high-energy hard worker. Some of these people may resent outside hires or hotshot trainees. Be humble.

6. **Final Meeting With the Decision-Maker.** You met him or her earlier in the morning, and he or she has probably already received feedback from subordinates regarding your potential. Express your interest and excitement. Mention something that was particularly impressive during the tour. It is critically important that you have a few questions ready because the decision-maker will undoubtedly say, "Do you have any final questions?" Recognize the professionalism and hospitality of the staff.

7. **Community Tour.** The host may personally escort you on a community tour to show housing, country clubs, etc., or may offer suggestions for you to tour the area the next day at your leisure. The facility visit required a tremendous amount of coordination and hard work on the part of the host. Recognize the effort and show your appreciation. Ask when and how you can expect to hear about the final decision.

Thank-You Letters

Not more than one day after a preliminary or selection interview, send a personalized letter to thank the interviewer(s). Don't just knock out a quick "Gee, thanks" letter, but rather develop a personal letter to enhance your chances of getting an offer. Correct spellings of the names and titles of those whom you met are mandatory—proofread the letter carefully; it must be perfect.

Sample Thank-You Letters

Dear Mr. Solter,

Thank you for the preliminary interview on December 12. As we discussed, I believe my background on the System 84 is directly applicable to your need for a technical liaison in the Process Control Department. Ameri-Can's track record is outstanding and the challenges and opportunities offered seem to be a direct match with my interests and capabilities. I am certainly interested in exploring the position further and look forward to hearing from you.

Dear Ms. Londers,

Thank you for the excellent facility visit on April 10. I appreciate the effort and planning that must have gone into such an efficiently organized day. I was particularly impressed with the Brand Management Division and the new project team approach that is being established.

The visit did nothing less than increase my interest in becoming a contributor at Ameri-Can, and I look forward to hearing from you. Please pass along my thanks to Mr. Richard Dalkins, Mr. Anthony Lopez, and Ms. Karen Rogers. Their input regarding a career with Ameri-Can was most beneficial to me. Thanks again.

Dear Mr. Hall,

I very much enjoyed our dinner meeting on March 28. I believe I can solve your traffic management problems and would welcome the challenges of the tasks we discussed. The management style of Ameri-Can is closely aligned with my own and I would expect a smooth and quick transition to your management team.

If I can provide any additional information please feel free to contact me at my office, 834-555-6744, or at home, 834-555-3378. Thank you for your consideration.

I suppose it is tempting to write a standard letter that looks the same for every interview; at least a lot of candidates go that route. Such a letter is viewed by recruiters as another "ho-hum" piece of mail and generates about as much excitement as a visit to Siberia. Invest some time in the letter and personalize it so that the recipient responds positively. Separate yourself from the competition.

Miscellaneous Interviewing Tips

Psychological Tests

Psychological tests serve the primary purpose of keeping psychologists off the street (they're known to drive 40 mph in the passing lane). Don't try to outguess the test questions. Answer them honestly and don't worry too much about the results. The employment decision will be based on the interview. Caution: If you are asked to draw a picture of your mother, don't draw a machete in her left hand. Don't worry about psychological tests.

Eye Contact

Maintain eye contact much as you would if you were having a conversation with a friend. Don't stare constantly to prove that you are not nervous. A fair amount of eye contact is all that is needed. Little or no direct eye contact will always generate a turndown because it implies a lack of confidence.

Comments About Employers

Never say anything negative about another company or a previous supervisor. Such comments will not serve to improve your chances of getting an offer and are considered poor taste in the book of interviewing etiquette.

Legal Considerations

There are many federal, state, and local laws, regulations, executive orders, and other directives affecting recruitment and interviewing. It is against the law to discriminate because of race, sex, religion, or national origin. Job candidates from age 40 to 70 are protected against age discrimination. Various kinds of affirmative action programs are required by employers who have government contracts. It is against the law to discriminate based on marital status . . . and the list goes on. What does this all mean to you in the interview?

If an interviewer asks a female candidate whether she is married or planning to get married he has violated the intent of protection under Title VII. Marital status legally should not be a factor in the decision. The job candidate has two options: (1) Reprimand the interviewer by telling him that the question is out of bounds, or (2) answer the question and assume that it is an innocent inquiry. It's your judgment.

Inexperienced interviewers may ask about your children or your age, etc. without any ill intent. You do have a right to point out the illegality of such questions, but must do so at the risk of generating a turndown. Within our legal system you would probably have to spend a lot of money and time to prove that a turndown was based on illegal discrimination. Furthermore, you must ask yourself whether you would want to work for a company that *really* was discriminating based on sex or race. Unless the question was an obvious and blatant case of discrimination, I would answer it and gamble that it arose out of inexperience or the interviewer's poor training, not out of willful discrimination. It's your call.

Conclusion

Knowing what to expect in the two types of interviews will enhance your interviewing effectiveness. Anxiety and nervousness are usually associated with an unknown, and you don't have that problem now. Practice answering each of the three types of interviewing questions and enjoy the interview as it proceeds (as you expect) through each step.

How to Prove Your Way to a Job Offer

6.1 INTRODUCTION

A job is in many ways a marriage between a company and a job candidate. A proposal is made, the offer accepted, and the "couple" is pronounced employer and employee. The two share common goals and responsibilities and strive to have a long-term, mutually beneficial (profitable) relationship. Before any such marriage can take place, though, the job candidate must address the problem of having an abbreviated "dating" period consisting of a brief thirty- to forty-five-minute interview, or at best a two-day visit. There is no time to get to know each other during a leisurely stroll along the beach or over a late-night cup of coffee at Perkins Restaurant. FACT: Companies base employment decisions on very brief glimpses of experience, qualifications, and potential. Considering that as much as 30 percent of the already brief interview time is spent verifying personal information (e.g., address), exchanging pleasantries, and discussing the company, *the job candidate actually only has a few minutes to convince the interviewer to extend an offer*. This chapter *teaches* you how to maximize those few minutes and prove that you should get the job offer. I emphasized the word "teaches" because this chapter could be cut down to four pages if my goal were simply to *tell* how to prove your way to a job offer. Read this chapter patiently and absorb each step before going on to the next. Learning and using the job search tool presented in this chapter will dramatically improve your interviewing success.

6.2   DETERMINE YOUR STRENGTHS

In order to convince the interviewer to propose an offer, you must *prove* that you have certain strengths that are prerequisites for the position the interviewer is seeking to fill. Determining the personal strengths in your repertoire is an important first step that warrants considerable attention and effort.

A strength is any personal factor that is required or viewed as a plus for a particular job: for example, leadership skills. Many candidates make the mistake of narrowly viewing strengths as *only* leadership skills, technical competency, grade point average, communication skills, etc., when actually strengths include a wide variety of factors ranging from dependability and adaptability to aggressiveness and friendliness. For example, if you were interviewing for a part-time position with a fast-food chain, dependability and friendliness might be the most important strengths required. The restaurant manager could care less about leadership ability; he only wants to know if you will regularly show up for work on Friday nights with a smile. Attention to detail is an important strength for a position as an office manager, working efficiently and quickly is important for a position as a construction worker, and having sensitivity is important for social work. Strengths include the complete spectrum of personal attributes associated with personality, experience, and qualifications.

You should spend a few hours reflecting on your own life experiences, qualifications, and personal traits to develop a personal inventory of strengths that are associated with a very special product: you.

You will undoubtedly have many strengths on your list, and undoubtedly an interviewer will not be interested in hearing about all of them. Having a safe driving record may be an important strength necessary to land a job as a truck driver, but obviously it should never arise in an interview for a position as a lab technician. Completion of your personal inventory of strengths leads to the next step in the process of proving your way to an offer: determining the strengths required by specific companies and for specific positions.

Common Strengths

Analytical Ability
Dependability
Friendliness
Ability to Think
  Conceptually
Enthusiasm
Ability to Get Results
Perseverance
Writing Skills
Loyalty
Thoroughness
Confidence
Bias for Action
Practical Approach
Hands-on Experience
Punctuality
Good Listening Skills
Self-Motivation
Technical Orientation
Professional Licenses
Social Poise
Common Sense
Ability to Pay Attention to
  Detail
Teaching Skills
Communication Skills
Sincerity
Team-Building Skills
Ability to Be a Team Player
Entrepreneurial Spirit
Persuasiveness
Honesty
Ability to Handle Pressure
Charisma

Experience in Field
Maturity
Idealism
Willingness to Work Hard
Ability to Solve Problems
Empathy
Negotiation Skills
Project Management Skills
Professional Memberships
Well-Rounded Back-
  ground
Ability to Relocate
Leadership
Sensitivity
Adaptability
Ability to Learn Quickly
Innovative Ideas
Competitiveness
Resourcefulness
Dedication
Patience
Discipline
Ethical Sense
Speaking Skills
Ambition
Pragmatism
Ability to Take Risks
Assertiveness
Independence
Good Grades
Outgoing Manner
Education
Energy
Special Training

6.3   DETERMINE THE COMPANY'S NEEDS

It is a waste of valuable interviewing time proving strengths that are of no interest to the interviewer. You may have worked hard for that high grade point average and certainly should be proud, but if you are interviewing for a practical, hands-on supervisory position, don't raise your G.P.A. up the flagpole. In that example, high grades are just a nice touch, not a primary selling point to get an offer. In fact, if you do emphasize high grades during that interview, the recruiter may feel that a design or technical position might be a better fit. It only makes sense that the required strengths must be identified before a candidate can prove that he is the best choice for the job. Your goal, then, is to gain a fairly good idea, before the interview, of which strengths are required to receive a particular job offer. It is not really difficult to determine general strengths that are important to a company and those that are required for a specific position; merge a little thought, common-sense analysis, and the following guidelines:

1.   Analyze the image and reputation of the company by studying the annual report and other literature. Question friends, placement officials, and the chamber of commerce to get an idea of the company's value system:
    a.   Is the company noted for innovation? Be prepared to prove that you are innovative.
    b.   Does the company have a family (paternalistic) atmosphere? Be prepared to prove that you are a team player.
    c.   Is the company initiating a major new quality program? Be prepared to prove that you are dedicated to quality production.
    d.   Is the company known for demanding long hours from new trainees? Be prepared to prove that you are ready and willing to work hard and long.

2. Job specifications/postings and job ads will allude to strengths that are required:
   a. "Mimimum 3.2 G.P.A." Prove technical competence.
   b. "Three years' experience required." They evidently want someone who can begin contributing immediately. Prove that you are competent in the field and a fast learner.
   c. "Supervisory experience required." Prove leadership skills.

3. Generic positions require certain standard strengths. With the assistance of a guidance or placement counselor, complete an analysis of the general standard strengths that are required for the position type(s) you are seeking. Following are general examples:
   a. Public accountant—ability to work well with people, strong communication skills, technical competence, enjoy extensive travel.
   b. Salesperson—persistence, excellent social skills, self-motivation, independence, outgoing and friendly personality.
   c. Teacher—planning and organizing skills, counseling skills, expertise in field, patience.
   d. Office clerk—dedication, loyalty, word processing skills, ability to be a team player, pleasant personality.
   e. Middle manager—proven track record, quantifiable achievements, leadership, planning skills.
   f. Manufacturing supervisor trainee—communication skills, leadership, hands-on practical nature, ability to work under pressure.
   g. Field engineer—communication skills, love of theory, love of hands-on work, leadership.

4. For each scheduled interview, find out the kind of recruiter you will be meeting (see Chapter 8). Identify the required strengths that are dictated by his or her biases.

5. Listen carefully to all questions during the interview. Relax as much as possible and think in terms of "What strength is this interviewer asking me to prove?"

    a. "Why did you sign up for this interview?"—Prove interest.
    b. "Have you always lived in the Midwest?"—Prove that you are adaptable and open for relocation.
    c. "Why did you decide to major in technology rather than engineering?"—Prove that you are logical and have clearly defined goals.
    d. "Have you ever worked shift work or weekends?"— Prove that you are dedicated and would have no problem working such a schedule.
    e. "What are your short-term and long-term goals?"— Prove vocational maturity.
    f. "How do you work under pressure and deadlines?"—Prove that you thrive on pressure and are results-oriented.

Knowing the required strengths provides a tremendous competitive edge in the interview. An entire evening could be spent discussing examples of job candidates who received turndowns because they wasted valuable interviewing time discussing strengths that were unimportant for the position.

Okay. Let's review what you've learned so far in this chapter:

1. You must spend a few hours developing a personal inventory of strengths.

2. Using the five guidelines, you must acquire a good understanding of the strengths that are important for each interview.

Building on those two points, we can now proceed to the primary topic: *how to prove to a recruiter that you have a particular strength.*

6.4   HOW TO PROVE A STRENGTH

Proving a strength is accomplished when the recruiter believes that, in fact, you do hold that strength. The process includes three steps:

Step I: State the strength you will prove.
Step II: Experience episode.
Step III: Tell what you have just proven.

We'll walk through each of the three steps in a SET using three examples that prove (A) leadership, (B) social poise, and (C) competence in field.

Step I: State the Strength You Will Prove

Telling the interviewer what you are going to prove will focus his attention and alert him that the next minute or two will provide key information necessary to support his final decision.

Example A.   *Recruiter:* "What is your greatest strength?" (Job candidate should prove the most important strength required for that particular position.)
Candidate: "My greatest strength is motivating and leading others to achieve a defined goal."

Example B.   *Recruiter:* "Our salespeople don't have much overnight travel, but there is a considerable amount of entertaining required." (Job candidate must prove that he or she offers the social poise necessary to successfully entertain customers in a variety of social and cultural environments.)
Candidate: "I believe that being close to customers is a critically important aspect of sales. I enjoy company and relate well to people from all types of backgrounds. Furthermore, I am interested in a broad spectrum of activities from golf to opera."

Example C.   *Recruiter:* "Do you think your grades equate to your ability?" (Job candidate is being asked to prove competence in field.)

Candidate: "I believe that grades do have a reasonable amount of validity in predicting ability and competence, but I also feel that experience carries equal value."

In the three preceding examples the candidate is *only stating the strengths* to be proved. It is important to understand that the candidate hasn't proved a thing! I emphasize this point because candidates often offer such responses as complete answers to questions. Consider Example B to illustrate my point. A recruiter has only a few minutes to decide whether it's worth spending $1,500 to pay this candidate's expenses for a second interview at a regional sales office. He must truly believe that the candidate has the social poise and skills necessary to entertain customers whose interests range from having a beer to attending an opera. The response in Example B proves nothing. The candidate is simply stating, "I can do it." *The recruiter will never make an offer based on your personal opinion of yourself or on a statement that is not validated by facts.* Literally every candidate interviewed will say, "I can do it." In the thousands of interviews I have conducted, rarely has a candidate answered a question with an admission of a weakness. A candidate would never say, "I don't think I would be comfortable entertaining in a fancy restaurant—I'm really a meat and potatoes person." No way! Everybody says, "I can do it" and interviewers are paid to sort out who really can and who really can't. You must offer substantive evidence to *prove* that you can do it. In Step II, the candidate demonstrates that he has the strength required.

Step II: Experience Episode

An experience episode is a short story drawn from your experience that effectively proves the strength and lends itself to easy recall by the recruiter. Experience episodes should take from thirty seconds to two minutes to present and *should be practiced prior to the interview.* The episode should be a concise, flowing mini-presentation that removes all doubt as to whether you actually have the strength or not. Whenever possible, include a quantifiable end result in the episode to enhance the dramatic impact; for example, "my action resulted in a 10 percent reduction in absenteeism," or "resulted in $4,000 savings." Use terminology that the interviewer can understand. You may know what an exponential curve is, but the recruiter may have never finished general business math. Continuing with the same three examples, the following experience episodes prove (A) leadership, (B) social poise, and (C) competence in field.

Example A: Experience Episode to Prove Leadership. "I have always had a high degree of energy and impatience to get things done. Others seem drawn by my enthusiasm, and I welcome taking on the leadership role. For example, I was elected chairman of the Homecoming Float Committee for three years in a row. I had the real challenge of supervising and coordinating the efforts of as many as fifty high school students to get the floats done on time. We received the first-place trophy for each of the three years—a record that still stands at the school. I continued gaining successful leadership experience during my college years as a class officer and as project leader for our senior project. In that project, I managed a team of eight engineering students with a prescribed goal to design and build a concrete boat. I think I played a key role in building a great team spirit, and a little bit of each of us went down when she was sunk to become a fish haven."

Comment: This experience episode offers concrete evidence that the candidate is a natural leader and increases the recruiter's confidence regarding a possible offer. The "quantified end result" of his leadership skills are three first-place trophies for class floats. Keep in mind that an experience episode doesn't have to be grandiose. Leadership can be proven with an experience episode drawn from Girl Scouts, school clubs, prior work experience, or volunteer work in the community. Simply relate a short, interesting story that offers substantive proof that you have the strength.

Example B: Experience Episode to Prove Social Skills.
"Personally, I think the requirement to entertain customers in

various cultural and social settings adds a real excitement to the sales process. A nice restaurant can certainly offer a complementary atmosphere in which to conduct business, and I appreciate a fine wine and excellent food presentation, but a pleasant round of golf or an evening of theater can be equally effective. The real purpose of entertainment is to leave the guest with a good feeling about the salesperson, the company, and the time spent together sharing a social experience. With a 12 handicap I can offer a good round of golf to any caliber player without risking embarrassment to a guest or myself. Also, as indicated on my resume, I enjoy a wide variety of interests; the entertainment function would just enhance my own quality of life."

Comment: The recruiter now feels comfortable that the candidate has the poise and confidence necessary to entertain in a variety of social settings. He knows that the candidate appreciates fine meals, is a pretty good golfer, and is sensitive to the guest's needs. The resume has offered further quantified evidence of the candidate's varied interests. The recruiter is convinced that the candidate meets his requirement regarding entertaining customers.

Don't be intimidated by this experience episode because you don't drink, hate theater, and are experienced only at miniature golf. You, as a unique individual, must draw from your own experiences to prove strengths. You might draw experience episodes from fraternity or sorority life, extracurricular activities, or previous work experience.

Example C: Experience Episode to Prove Competence. "As you can see from my resume, I have a 3.1 grade point average. I worked hard for the grades and am proud of my academic record. The grades demonstrate an achieved level of technical understanding in marketing, but I believe the real strength that I offer is the ability to take the theory and book learning and apply the knowledge in a business environment. Last summer I worked as an intern at Ajax Company—they manufacture more than fifty different kinds of kitchen utensils. I was assigned to the advertising/brand management division to assist in the release of a new product. The marketing study I completed was used to determine the testing area demographics. I received an outstanding rating at the end of the summer and in fact have received an offer from Ajax to enter their training program. By the way, the product has been very successful and is projected to represent 2 percent of sales by the third quarter next year."

Comment: The candidate proved competence. Her grade point average, experience in the field, successful marketing study, and job offer from Ajax offer substantive evidence that serves to convince the recruiter that she is, in fact, competent in her field. The successful new product release quantifies her competency and the experience episode lends itself to easy recall. A week after the interview the recruiter is reviewing his files and remembers, "Oh yes, she was the candidate who helped Ajax release a new product that is doing very well now. As I recall, she also is holding an offer from them. I think we should extend an offer ASAP."

Step III: Tell the Interviewer What You Have Proved.

The final step of a SET ties the knot in the process by *telling* the interviewer what has just been proven. You have probably heard that in public speaking you should tell the audience what you're going to say, say it, and then tell them what you've said. The same logic applies here. Telling the interviewer what has just been proved reinforces the point and serves as an effective closure and transition statement for the candidate or the interviewer to put another question on the table.

Example A. "To summarize, I believe these examples show that my greatest strength is leadership to motivate others to achieve prescribed goals."

Example B. "The entertainment function of the position would be a real pleasure, not a chore."

Example C. "I feel confident that my formal training and the solid field experience I have discussed prove my technical competence to achieve results."

We have looked at each of the three steps required to prove a strength:

Step I: State the strength you will prove.
Step II: Experience episode
Step III: Tell what has just been proven.

Putting the three steps together in a concise mini-presentation (SET) will dramatically improve interviewing success. Examine our three examples with all three steps put together in a SET (note the transition through each step).

Example A: SET to Prove Leadership.   "My greatest strength is motivating and leading others to achieve a defined goal. I have always had a high degree of energy and impatience to get things done. For example, I was elected chairman of the Homecoming Float Committee for three years in a row. I had the real challenge of supervising and coordinating the efforts of as many as fifty high school students to get the floats done on time. We received the first-place trophy for each of the three years—a record that still stands at the school. I continued gaining successful leadership experience during my college years as a class officer and as a project leader for our senior project. In that project I managed a team of eight engineering students whose prescribed goal was to design and build a concrete boat. I think I played a key role in building a great team spirit, and a little bit of each of us went down when she was sunk to become a fish haven. To summarize, I believe that these examples show that my greatest strength is leadership to motivate others to achieve prescribed goals."

Example B: SET to Prove Social Poise Necessary to Entertain Customers   "I believe that being close to customers is a critically important aspect of sales. I enjoy the company of a wide variety of personality types and a broad spectrum of activities from golf to opera. Personally, I think the requirement to entertain customers in various cultural and social settings adds real excitement to the sales process. A nice restaurant can certainly offer a complementary atmosphere in which to conduct business, and I appreciate a fine wine and excellent food presentation, but a pleasant round of golf or an evening of theater can be equally effective. The real purpose of entertainment is to leave the guest with a good feeling about the salesperson, the company, and the time spent together sharing a social experience. With a 12 handicap, I can offer a good round of golf to any caliber player without risking embarrassment to a guest or myself. Also, as indicated on my resume, I enjoy a wide variety of interests; the entertainment function would just enhance my own quality of life. The entertainment function of the sales position would be a real pleasure, not a chore."

Example C: SET to Prove Competence in Field   "I believe that grades do have a reasonable amount of validity in predicting ability and competence, but I also feel that experience carries equal value. As you can see from my resume, I have a 3.1 grade point average. The grades demonstrate an achieved level of technical understanding in marketing, but I believe the real strength I have to offer is the ability to take the theory and book learning and apply the knowledge in a business environment. Last summer I worked as an intern at Ajax Company—they manufacture more than fifty different kinds of kitchen utensils. I was assigned to the advertising/brand management division to assist in the release of a new product. The marketing study I completed was used to determine the testing area demographics. I received an outstanding rating at the end of the summer and in fact have received an offer from Ajax to enter their training program. By the way, the product has been very successful and is projected to represent 2 percent of sales by the third quarter of next year. I feel confident that my formal training and the solid field experience I have discussed prove my technical competence to achieve results."

Conclusion

Using SETS to substantiate and prove that you offer certain strengths is a powerful tool that clearly separates you from the competition. Have you ever been interviewed for a position that you knew you could handle and would enjoy and yet still received a turndown? Have you ever wondered why you received a turndown from an interview that went well? *Unless required strengths are proven, the interviewer will never extend an offer.*

You should develop and practice several SETS that prove the strengths you offer. They should not be memorized, but rather should flow naturally in a conventional manner during the interview. A SET can often be modified slightly to prove many different strengths. For example, the job candidate who used the float-building experience episode could slightly modify the SET and use it to prove ability to work as a team player.

SETS should be brief, concise, and focused to ensure that the interviewer is convinced that you do, in fact, offer that strength. Few candidates realize the importance of proving *required* strengths. You are now one of the few—congratulations.

7

How to Handle Liabilities
in an Interview

7.1 INTRODUCTION

In this chapter we'll examine the more difficult and unpleasant
flip side of the interview coin: how to handle liabilities in an
interview. What do you say if you have lousy grades or weak
job experience? What should you do or say if the interviewer
knows that you were laid off or, even worse, fired from your
last job? How should you explain the fact that you are seeking
to change your career path? Each of us has liabilities, and how
they are handled in an interview is a primary factor in the decision-making process. This chapter presents a powerful interviewing tool to neutralize the negative effect of a liability and
actually turn it into a positive asset. Sound impossible? Read
on.

7.2 NO EXCUSES

*A liability is any personal factor or experience that hinders the
chances of getting an offer for a particular job.* Think about that
definition for a moment, because it places the term "liability"
in a much broader context than is usually granted by most job
seekers. The definition implies that the same personal attrib-
ute that is considered a strength by some companies for par-

ticular positions may be viewed as a liability by others. For example, having straight A's and extensive experience (over-qualified) can be strengths for certain positions and liabilities for others. A mature job candidate's excellent experience may very well be considered a liability for a position as a management trainee and a strength for a position as a general supervisor. On the other hand, there is nothing wrong with having a C average or limited work experience, but when interviewing for certain positions, these too can be liabilities or strengths. *A liability is just a part of who you are and should never be handled in an apologetic manner during any aspect of the job search process.*

I know of nothing that turns a recruiter off more than a sob story or an apology for a liability. *Don't ever say this:*

"I know I only have a C average, but I think it is important for you to know that I worked twelve hours per week and was heavily involved in campus extracurricular activities."

"I really wish I could have gotten a job in my field, but the economy was just so bad and there was absolutely nothing available. I put in applications at more than twenty companies and didn't even get one interview."

"I have always wanted to work in industry, but with my degree in education I was limited to teaching in high school."

Now, before getting upset because you believe that the excuses are valid, understand that immediately following the interview in which the excuses are offered, in walks a candidate who worked *thirty* hours per week and still managed to achieve a B+ average! Following is a candidate who somehow managed to land a tremendous summer job in his field in spite of the economy! *Excuses, sob stories, and apologies for liabilities will never improve your chances of success in an interview.* (Sorry.) The success or failure of any business relies on one thing: results. There is no excuse column when computing the bottom line. Show that you are ready to play the game "Careering for Dollars" by not presenting any excuses or apologies in the interview.

If we were sitting together discussing this topic right now, you might be saying, "Hey, wait a minute. What *should* I say about my low grades? I didn't have any summer jobs because I worked for my Dad. What about the sickness in my family that caused a big drop in my grades last semester? Sure, I have been a teacher for ten years, but shouldn't I explain how I have always been interested in working in industry?" This chapter will offer answers to those and similar questions, but first it is necessary to understand a little bit more about the nature of liabilities.

7.3 WHAT IS YOUR GREATEST WEAKNESS?

Liabilities are often referred to as "weaknesses." In fact, one of the most common questions used in interviewing is, "In your opinion, what is your greatest weakness?" This is a great question for interviewers because many times a candidate will reveal a basic flaw that serves as justification for the turndown. For example, candidates have admitted to me that they freeze under the pressure of tests, are procrastinators, or have an indecisive nature. Their honesty and openness cannot be questioned, but neither can the fact that a turndown will be on the way. Without compromising integrity or honesty, answer the question by offering a "positive" weakness:

> "I suppose if I were to describe my greatest weakness it would be that I am impatient to get things done. I am very much results-oriented and am rather uncomfortable until an assigned job is done."

Impatience is a "positive" weakness that will not generate a turndown. Understand that what is really happening with this question is that the interviewer is tossing out some bait to see if he can find something that warrants a turndown. Don't even nibble. Respond with a weakness that will enhance your chances of receiving an offer. Following are a few examples of positive weaknesses that may apply to you:

1. *Impatient* to get the job done.

2. Expect the same high level of *dedication* and *strong work ethic* in others.

3. Difficulty separating work from play—*really enjoy working* (borderline workaholic).

4. *Somewhat agressive*—if I see a job to be done, I do it.

5. *Sensitive to others' needs* to the point that I sometimes think I should be a diplomat.

7.4   DETERMINE YOUR LIABILITIES

To determine your strengths you invested a number of hours of reflection to develop a personal inventory of all of those positive attributes associated with *you*: one heck of a job candidate. It is just as important, though, to recognize your liabilities. Ask yourself the question, "What is there about me or my background that could work against my receiving a job offer?" If you can't think of any, ask a parent or in-law. *Everyone* has liabilities. I'll help you get started (notice I said *started*) by listing some common liabilities:

Inexperience	Overqualification
Youth	Maturity
Overspecialization	Generalization
Same Job for Many Years	History of "Job-Hopping"
Lack of a Degree	High-Powered M.B.A.
Low Grades	Extremely High Grades
Current Unemployment	Employment in Different
Fired from a Job	Field
Liberal Arts Degree/Seeking	Layoff from Previous Job
Industry Position	Technical Degree/Seeking
High Current Earnings	Management Position
	Low Current Earnings

In summary, remember the definition of liability: "something about you that works against your receiving a *particular* job offer." A liability for one job may be a strength for another; for example, maturity can be a strength or a liability depending on the company and the particular job. Prepare for each interview by analyzing which strengths and liabilities will be critical. Now that you have a solid understanding of the nature of liabilities, I'll answer the question posed earlier in the chapter: "What should you say about liabilities during an interview?"

7.5   HOW TO HANDLE A LIABILITY IN AN INTERVIEW

Maybe you goofed around in college and have low grades, or have an engineering degree and three solid years' experience as a waiter, or after twenty years with one company have been laid off; my friend, you have a liability that can be the primary reason for a turndown. If not handled correctly, a single liability can outweigh all of your strengths and generate a standard "No thank you" letter. The following three-step procedure will neutralize the negative effect of a liability and significantly improve your chances of getting a job offer. Each step will be explained using three examples of liabilities: (A) lack of experience, (B) low grades, and (C) age.

Step I: Recognize the liability as a legitimate issue or concern.

Step II: Identify the strength that is perceived by the interviewer as missing.

Step III: Use a SET to prove that you have that strength.

Step I: Recognize the Liability as a Legitimate Issue or Concern

Interviewers are often just as uncomfortable asking about liabilities as you are about being asked. Put yourself in my shoes when I must ask, "Why weren't you involved in any campus activities?" For all I know, maybe it is because you are withdrawn or perhaps a loner. When an interviewer begins delving into liabilities, it is an intrusion that leads to at least the border of the candidate's most personal characteristics. This is especially uncomfortable when considering the fact that the interviewer and candidate have known each other for only a few minutes!

Set the interviewer at ease by recognizing the liability question as a legitimate concern. This will serve as an icebreaker for both you and the recruiter. Let the interviewer know that you think it is perfectly legitimate to ask about the liability. The following examples show how a candidate can set an interviewer at ease when being questioned about a liability.

Example A (lack of experience):   "Your job specification stated that the position requires three years of experience in purchasing, and I think it is a legitimate concern that my experience has been in finance."

Example B (low grades):   "I believe that the fact that I did not set any scholastic records by achieving a C average is a legitimate concern of all potential employers. As you know, there are a lot of variables reflected in my G.P.A., but it is a valid point of discussion."

Example C (age):   "I have found that my maturity and many years of experience quite often raise legitimate questions and concerns."

Comments: In each of the example responses, the candidate is setting the recruiter at ease. Once the legitimacy of the concern has been confirmed, proceed to Step II.

Step II: Identify the Strength That Is Perceived as Missing

Each liability implies that a strength is missing. For example, low grades imply that the strength "Technical Competence" is missing. Inexperience in the field implies that the strength "Ability to Contribute Quickly Without Much Training" is missing. *After the candidate recognizes the legitimacy of concern about a liability, he must identify the strength that the interviewer perceives as missing in his background.* This step moves the liability a notch away from negative toward the positive end of the scale. Admittedly, this concept requires a little bit of mind stretching, but the three following examples should help ease the task:

Example A (lack of experience): *Perceived missing strength*: ability to contribute quickly without the benefit of extensive training.

"I can see that this position requires an individual who must immediately contribute as a purchasing agent without the luxury of an extensive training or learning period. He must begin immediately to work with the vendors and department heads to effectively service your new facility start-up that is scheduled to go on-line this fall. Is that a correct assessment?"

Example B (low grades): *Perceived missing strength*: technical competence.

"The training program you described seems to require a strong foundation in practical application of marketing theory. It would seem that a strength in statistics would be particularly valuable. Is that an accurate observation?"

Example C (age): *Perceived missing strength*: ability to work long hours, commitment to a career, enthusiasm.

"My experience says that the position of office manager supervising five clerks will require a person with a lot of drive, spirit, and a willingness to work long hours to ensure the effective operation of the office."

Comment: In each of the previous examples, the candidate has identified the missing strength. The lack of experience is *not* the real concern. The interviewer's real concern is that the candidate will require a lot of training before he can begin to contribute. The low grades of the candidate are *not* the real concern. The interviewer's real concern is that the candidate does not have the technical or theoretical base necessary to succeed in the job. The age of the candidate is *not* the real concern. The interviewer is concerned about the candidate's ability and drive to work long hours for many years to come. This is a very important concept for job seekers, and if you understand the following statements, you've passed the test. A company may require a certain college degree because that degree indicates that the candidate can probably do a particular thing that the company needs. Even if you don't have that degree, if you can prove that you can do that thing, you will get the job. *Zero in on the real concern and then prove that you have what it takes.*

Step III: Use a SET to Prove That You Have That Strength

In Step 1, you recognized the liability question as a legitimate concern. The interviewer and the candidate were set at ease. In Step II, you identified the missing strength. You've shown tremendous insight by recognizing what the recruiter is *really* concerned about. In Step III, the final transition from negative to positive is accomplished by using a SET to prove the underlying strength that the recruiter has perceived as missing.

Example A: Use a SET to prove the capability to immediately begin to contribute.

Example B: Use a SET to prove technical competence in marketing.

Example C: Use a SET to prove ability to work long hours for many years to come.

Summary

You must practice handling liabilities before the interview. Practice will reduce anxiety and play a key role in improving interviewing success. Each of the steps in the process will complement each other as you field a liability question, neutralize it, and then hammer home with a SET to prove the perceived missing strength. As you read the complete three-step procedure in our three following examples, identify each of the steps and note the smooth transition from negative to positive.

Example A (lack of experience): The recruiter has raised the issue of this liability by saying, "I notice that your background is in finance. How will that apply to our needs for an assistant purchasing agent?"

"I know that your job specification stated that the position requires three years of purchasing experience, and I think it is a legitimate concern that my experience has been in accounting and administration. From our discussion I can see that this position requires an individual who must immediately contribute as an assistant purchasing agent without the luxury of an extensive training period. He must begin immediately to work with the vendors and department heads to effectively service your new facility start-up, which is scheduled to go online this fall. Is that an accurate assessment?

"I believe that many of my skills in administration will directly transfer to the purchasing functions and will facilitate my contributing immediately to your start-up. As an accountant I serviced all levels of management and developed strong communication skills in dealing with department heads. Last summer I assisted each of our ten departments in developing a planning budget for all material resources. Projecting the needs for a wide variety of departments required close coordination and negotiations as we were under a tight budget situation. The plans came in 15 percent under last year's budget and helped contribute to record profits. My experience in tracking costs will also directly transfer to meet your requirements. I processed purchase orders from initial letter of intent to receipt and payment, using an IBM PC. Last year's disbursements totaled over $150,000. My proven skills in material management, communications with all levels of management, and cost tracking and my hands-on familiarity with computer systems will enable me to begin contributing immediately as an assistant purchasing agent. Your annual report indicated that Ameri-Can is decentralizing many business functions. Does that include purchasing?"

Comment: This candidate *had* a real problem liability. He was seeking a job in purchasing, but only had accounting experience. He knew that this liability might come up in the interview and was ready with the three-step procedure. Notice how the candidate took an extremely negative liability and smoothly directed it to the perceived missing strength.

Example B (low grades): The recruiter has brought up the issue of low grades by saying, "We are particularly interested in employing someone who can offer a strong background in market research. Your grades would seem to indicate that a better match might be in advertising or management."

"I believe the fact that I did not set any scholastic records by achieving a C average is a legitimate concern of all potential employers. As you know, there are a lot of variables reflected in any G.P.A., but it is a valid point of discussion. The training program you described seems to require a strong foundation in practical application of marketing theory. I would think that a strength in statistics would be particularly valuable. Is that an accurate observation?

"I have always enjoyed statistics and have completed three courses each having a heavy emphasis in analysis. For my senior project, I completed a research study of ten major factors of consumer awareness regarding the deregulation of natural gas. I received an A on the project and recently submitted it to Exxon Corporation for their review. Last summer I worked as an intern for the business department and did a marketing study to determine the practicality of offering an M.B.A. program on our sister campuses. The board decided against the program based, at least in part, on my study. I believe that one of my greatest strengths is the ability to take the theories of marketing, compile statistical data, and derive conclusions that form a base for business decisions."

Comment: This candidate knew that low grades would be a factor in this particular interview. He practiced how he would handle the liability and even has more SETS in his back pocket if the recruiter gives an indication that he is still not comfortable with the grade problem.

Example C (age):   Everyone knows that it is against federal law for employers to discriminate based on age. Nevertheless, I present age as an example of a liability because the transformation of the American economic structure is displacing thousands of older workers who must re-enter the job market and who, in spite of those federal laws, face discrimination. An interviewer will be careful to never directly mention a concern regarding age, but rather might say something like: "This job will require a lot of overtime and hard work. You already have more than twenty years of experience as an office manager; are you ready to commit yourself to a new career effort of this magnitude?"

"I have found that my maturity and many years of experience quite often raise legitimate questions and concerns. I know that the position of office manager supervising five clerks will require a person with a lot of drive, spirit, and a willingness to work long hours to ensure the efficient operation of the office. I am ready and able.

"I am in excellent health and exercise regularly at the YMCA. In fact, for the last year, I have attended an early-bird fitness program of swimming and jogging that meets from 6:30 to 7:30 three mornings each week. I have always taken pride in staying in good physical shape and have not missed a single day of work for the past five years. I thrive on keeping busy and working hard. If you have any questions regarding my commitment to work for many years to come, let me add that I have two children in college and one more to go. Quite honestly, you will not find a more hard-working, dedicated, and enthusiastic office manager. I see my many years of experience as just an added plus that will allow me to contribute immediately."

7.6   HOW INTERVIEWERS ASK ABOUT LIABILITIES

Recruiters rarely ask directly about liabilities; therefore, active listening is required during the interview to determine when a liability is being brought up. An important point to understand is that if a recruiter *does* ask about a liability, he is providing an opportunity for you to prove that you have the perceived missing strength. *If the recruiter did not even bother to bring up an obvious serious liability, there is a good possibility that a turndown will follow.* A candidate who leaves an interview and says, "Phew! I wasn't even asked about not ever having a job over the past four summers. Boy, was I lucky," did not luck out, but rather struck out. A turndown will be arriving in the mail shortly. Seize upon questions about liabilities as opportunities to succeed in the interview. If you have a very obvious serious liability that the recruiter has not mentioned, you must invoke common sense and decide whether to bring it up yourself and use the three-step procedure or conclude that it is not a primary factor in the interview. (I never said interviewing was a piece of cake.) Be pleased when liabilities are mentioned in an interview. It means the recruiter is interested enough to provide an opportunity for you to prove that you have the perceived missing strength. Following are examples of statements and questions that are used to bring up liabilities indirectly:

1. "This job will require some weekend and shift work." (Too old, vocational immaturity, or not committed to a career.)

2. "Why didn't you take any statistics courses?" (Low G.P.A., not competent in field.)

3. "Were you ever involved in any leadership positions?" (No leadership potential.)

4. "I see you were a lifeguard for three summers—interesting." (Weak experience, possibly weak ambition.)

5. "We were really seeking a marketing major." (Lack of technical competence.)

6. "I see you have had a lot of experience with many different companies. (Unstable, job-hopper.)

7. "So, how long have you been unemployed?" (Lack of competence or ambition.)

8. "I see that you have never really worked in this field."
   (Vocational immaturity, lack of interest or competence.)

Conclusion

Handling liabilities in an interview is one of the most challenging aspects of the job search process. Few candidates are able to discuss liabilities without avoiding a turndown and many candidates fail to recognize when a liability is being brought up. You are no longer in that category. The three-step process will improve effectiveness in every interviewing situation from part-time gas pump jockey to management traineee to director of sales engineering. You can now stand apart from your competition and take another step toward achieving a clear-cut competitive edge.

8

Five Kinds of Interviewers: How to Succeed with Each

8.1 INTRODUCTION

Books, articles, and workshops about interviewers have fostered a totally inaccurate image of a vague, possibly hostile entity who has been cast as a key player in your destiny, even though the role is in a short one-act play (called an interview) lasting perhaps only thirty minutes. This mysterious and generally unknown "actor" flies into your town late at night and then appears in a windowless eight-foot-by-six-foot cubicle on the next morning to do "what he does" to you. Even worse, you may have to travel to an office complex and be ushered down a long corridor with your footsteps echoing behind you as you approach the door to his "lair."

You have prepared for the meeting by learning about such frightfully important areas as:

"How to answer tough questions."
"How to write a resume that wins attention."
"How to dress for the interview."
"How to deal with the unexpected in an interview."

After all of the above, it is no wonder that candidates often feel as though they are walking into Vincent Price's horror chamber rather than into an interviewing room or office. If I had to prepare for an interview with myself, the way I am written about, I too would be a nervous wreck!

This chapter humanizes the interviewer by discussing and analyzing the five major kinds of interviewers that you may, on occasion, have to deal with either on campus or during a plant trip or office visit. Understanding the needs, biases, and idiosyncrasies of each type of recruiter or interviewer will serve as a subtle but powerful tool to improve your interviewing success. Also, this chapter should alter that unrealistic and vague image you have of interviewers and replace it with one that corresponds more closely to fact. Interviewers are quite often someone's next-door neighbor!

8.2 WHY YOU MUST UNDERSTAND THE RECRUITER AS A HUMAN BEING

Whenever you enter a relationship or dialogue with some-one in which you expect to negotiate something, receive ap-proval or support, or—in the case of a recruiter—receive a job offer, it is definitely to your advantage to *understand the needs and requirements of the person with whom you are dealing*. Most job candidates practice this methodology in normal day-to-day situations, but rarely use it in the most critical arena, the job interview.

For example, if you want to receive an A from a professor it helps to know her specific requirements. Learning how much emphasis is placed on books as opposed to lectures, the types of questions that will be asked on tests, her lecture style, etc., gives a student a distinct competitive edge in the classroom. You need that same competitive edge to receive an A rating from the interviewer. *Each recruiter is overflowing with personal biases, idiosyncrasies, prejudices, preferences, and a particular personal concept of what it takes to receive an offer*. Understand-ing that fact alone and allowing it to affect your interviewing strategy will improve your offer-to-interview ratio. Although each recruiter is a unique person with a unique set of biases, it is fairly easy to stereotype interviewers into five major cate-gories:

1. Young Fast-Tracker (YFT)

2. Middle Manager (M&M)

3. Technical Person (TP)

4. Your Future Boss (FB)

5. Professional Interviewer (PRO)

8.3 YOUNG FAST-TRACKER

Quite often a young employee is rewarded for the great job he or she is doing by being sent to interview *YOU*. Many times the YFT is designated to recruit at his alma mater, which explains why YFTs most often interview on Mondays and Fridays (it facilitates a weekend visit with old friends). The recruiting trip is viewed as an interesting diversion, a new challenge, and a company-paid trip to the old stomping grounds. It would be inaccurate to imply that a YFT would do anything less than his typical best, but his best is severely limited by a general gross lack of interviewing experience that directly affects you, the interviewee. Your interview strategy should reflect the fact that the YFT is a rookie. Before examining a few interviewing techniques that complement the YFT's inexperience, let's quickly identify the criteria that determine when, in fact, you have a YFT sitting at the desk across from you.

Recognizing the YFT

The YFT is unusually well groomed, conservatively dressed, early to mid twenties, possibly preppy, happy and outgoing (after all, this assignment is a prize), *loves* the company, *loves* the school, and is most likely experienced in social activities. Often the YFT looks as though he or she stepped out of a Sears spring catalog. Need I say more? No, but why not? If there is ever any doubt about whether the recruiter is a YFT, just ask one or more of the following questions:

1. "Did you graduate from this school?" YFT response: "Yes, just a few years ago."

2. "How long have you been with the company?" YFT response: (Six or less years).

3. "Have you got tickets for tonight's game?" YFT response: "Yes, fifty yard line."

4. "Are you a full-time interviewer?" YFT response: "No, I recruit only on an as-needed basis."

Recognizing the young fast-tracker requires the absolute minimum of perceptual skills—it's like distinguishing an old pair of sneakers from a pair of docksiders.

The YFT and the Interview

The YFT has *maybe* been through a brief workshop on interviewing, but at best is *grossly inexperienced* as an interviewer. His or her base of reference for comparing you to the norm is very narrow and probably statistically invalid. *He doesn't know whether you are an outstanding, above average, or average candidate because he simply has no frame of reference.* You should be thinking, "How can this YFT evaluate me fairly?" Allow me to briefly climb up on a soapbox to say that in the world of employment selection, fairness is a fast-moving target—take a shot, take your pick. The YFT will compare you to the only base reference he is sure about: *himself.* He will evaluate and select candidates based on how similar the candidate is to his primary benchmark. Don't be too critical, because in a few years you may be doing the same thing.

How to Get an Offer From a YFT

To receive an offer from a YFT, the interviewee simply must exhibit interests, traits, skills, goals, and experiences to which the YFT can relate. Use common sense in determining the requirements of a specific YFT, but following is a list of general categories that will often carry significant evaluatory weight with a YFT:

1. Extracurricular activities

2. Common interest in fraternity/sorority, sports, school activities, hobbies, etc.

3. Enthusiasm, leadership positions on campus, club officer, etc.

4. Admiration for and proven interest in his or her company

5. Self-confidence, friendliness, well-rounded background

6. Enthusiasm (listed twice for emphasis)

Since the YFT is an inexperienced interviewer, you should play an assertive, active role in helping him through the interview. Don't let him talk sports or old times on campus too long. He only has a few minutes to decide if you are enough like him to receive a job offer. Be ready for the standard training-manual questions, such as, "What is your greatest weakness?" There is a possibility that he is more nervous than you—make him comfortable by asking many questions. YFTs will be too reticent to bring up your liabilities for fear of creating an embarrassing situation. If you have an obvious liability that you know will concern the YFT, diplomatically mention it and handle it with the three-step procedure outlined in Chapter 7, "How to Handle Liabilities in an Interview."

8.4   MIDDLE MANAGER

The middle manager, M&M, is a conservative, successful employee who places a high priority on hiring the "right stuff" to serve his company's future managerial needs. He believes in developing young talent and promoting from within. His lack of interviewing expertise is compensated for by a business acumen that has been developed through years of trial and error. He enjoys the interviewing assignment, but is anxious to get back to the work that is piling up on his desk. A serious demeanor supported by a paternal instinct makes for a rather pleasant interview. The only exception is the "old school" manager who still believes in the anachronistic stress interview. Presenting a business problem during a thirty-minute interview or asking stress questions such as, "What would you do if. . . ?" is on the borderline of absurdity. In such a stress interview, try to relax and don't look intimidated.

Recognizing the M&M is almost as simple as identifying the YFT. Standard-issue highly polished wing tips, gray hair, rumpled, expensive suit, ten to twenty-five years with the company, serious demeanor and a strictly business attitude say it all. There are very few female M&Ms because, relatively speaking, there are (unfortunately) few female middle managers.

How to Get an Offer From a Middle Manager

The Middle Manager values:

1. Work ethic

2. Grades

3. Knowledge of company

4. Confidence

5. Vocational maturity

6. Dedication

7. Humility

8. Willingness to "pay dues" (that is, to start at the bottom)

9. Leadership

Don't ever ask an M&M about vacation eligibility or benefits! Three summers as a lifeguard on the Jersey shore will not impress the middle manager. He is looking for drive, ambition, and dedication to hard work. Talk about the part-time job that helped pay for your education in order to strike a positive nerve.

Expect philosophical questions such as, "Where do you expect to be in five years?" and, "Tell me about yourself." Let him control the interview while you concentrate on proving that you have the required strengths to receive an offer from a middle manager.

8.5   TECHNICAL PERSON

A number of companies will have technical representatives conduct interviews at least partially based on the assumption that it takes one to know one. Like the YFT, the TP will usually have very little interviewing training or experience. He is armed instead with a mission to seek out one of his brothers or sisters in accounting, engineering, marketing, etc. The TP often loves his field of expertise as much as or maybe more than the company.

While the YFT is calling on old friends during his visit to campus, the TP is visiting a professor or a laboratory sink that still has special meaning.

The title of the TP is often the only indicator needed to recognize this interview type: analyst, marketing assistant, special engineer, design engineer, buyer, technical representative, etc. If you don't know the title, simply ask. If you don't ask, look to see if he has a Bic pen and a mechanical pencil in his pocket; this is a sure tip-off. *A technical person will often have the narrowest selection criteria of all interviewer types.* His primary focus will be on technical competence.

How to Get an Offer From a Technical Person

Since the TP is not an interviewer by trade, you must take an assertive stance in helping him through the interview. His evaluation will emphasize such factors as:

1.   Grade point average

2.   Interest and knowledge in field

3.   Special academic achievements in field

4   Caliber of your school's program

If the TP is not a graduate of your school, he may be biased against your school's program and curriculum. Play it safe and use a SET (see Chapter 6) to prove your school's credentials in your technical discipline. Prove technical competence in order to receive an offer from a TP.

8.6   YOUR FUTURE BOSS

Occasionally you may interview with an actual department head who is specifically interested in finding someone to work for him. A lot of managers would just as soon *not* let some "personnel guy" do it. After all, "Who could do a better job selecting my assistant than myself?" The FB has a specific idea of what he wants to see in a job candidate and the attributes vary depending on the FB's management philosophy. For example, the autocratic FB wants an employee who will keep his nose to the grindstone and take directions without questions, while the participative FB is searching for leadership indicators and a mature professional sensitivity to others. Listen closely to his statements and questions to get a feel for his management style. Ask questions such as:

"What is the management philosophy of (company)?"
"What are new management trainees directly accountable for in the first two years?"
"What are you seeking in a solid candidate for this position?"

Recognizing Your Future Boss

The FB has been with the company from four to twenty years and may or may not be a fast-tracker. If he has fifteen years of service and is still in lower management, he is probably an FB who has peaked out. This is important for you to know, because if you emphasize your lofty ambition to run the company, it may be viewed as immaturity (remember that he wasn't able to come close to that goal). Only a few employees ever attain upper management. Most of us will end up with a barbecue pit, 2.1 children, and—you're not going to like this one—a station wagon. Seriously, I have a Chevrolet station wagon with a tilt steering wheel. It's great for hauling my 2.1 kids. If you are not sure whether the interviewer is an FB simply ask, "Will I report to you in this position?"

How to Get an Offer From an FB

The FB will give significant weight to:

1. Vocational maturity

2. Common sense

3. Practical perspective as opposed to idealism

4. Traditional work ethic

5. Work experience

6. Ability to be a team player

7. Positive attitude, humble demeanor

I recall interviewing a recent graduate from a major university, which I will not name but whose initials are "N.D.," who said, "I want to become President of the United States, but first I need some work experience." Be level-headed, sincere, and practical in order to receive an offer from your future boss.

8.7 PROFESSIONAL RECRUITER/INTERVIEWER

A professional recruiter (PRO) is a person who makes a living interviewing job seekers. Think about that for a second or two. An individual whose primary activity in life is interviewing people like you day after day, year after year. A person whose life is a series of airplane rides, motel rooms, maps, dinners at Howard Johnson's place, and interviews. It is a difficult and demanding profession, but the flight layovers and hectic travel schedule are somehow balanced by the beautiful drive from Cal-Berkeley to Stanford. The winter blizzard at Michigan Tech is remembered with fondness and the pioneer spirit of those great people living on the Upper Peninsula is inspirational. Recruiters are modern-day pioneers exploring each college's unique academic world.

Outsiders with a shallow perspective might see interviewing thousands of job candidates as boring drudgery, but each interviewee brings a brand new set of life experiences and traits that must be explored and evaluated. Each interview is new.

Recruiters' backgrounds are as diverse as the graduates they interview, but sensitivity, understanding, and a pragmatic attitude that separates emotion from business sense are basic traits resident in most PROs.

Recognizing the PRO

Professional recruiters hold position titles such as college relations representative, personnel representative, recruiter, and staffing specialist. PROs look like car salesmen for a Mercedes dealership. As a professional representative for a company, a PRO is expected to present a polished professional image.

It is critical to your interviewing strategy that you know when you are dealing with a PRO. If you aren't sure what a Mercedes salesman looks like, ask a question that will lead to the information you need:

"Is this your first visit to our campus?" A PRO probably has visited your school many times.

"Are you a professional recruiter?"

"Do you work in personnel?"

The PRO and the Interview

The PRO has interviewed thousands of candidates and has a solid benchmark for "average," "good," and "outstanding." The interview will be controlled by the PRO, who will probably have you speaking 80 percent of the time. The PRO is interviewing to evaluate you, not to share his wisdom on a particular topic.

Listen carefully to each question because the PRO is looking for a response that will facilitate his evaluation in a particular rating catagory. Questions will rarely be wasted. Understand that he is taking his best shot to screen you *out*, not screen you *in*. The PRO considers the interview a business conversation between two equals. Don't be ingratiating or subservient in attitude. He must be convinced that you can positively influence his company's bottom line. PROs are searching for an excellent potential return on investment. Your overall rating is equivalent to an ROI.

How to Get an Offer From a PRO

To receive an offer from a PRO requires a great rating in each of the seven evaluatory categories. If you fail to achieve a solid rating in any one of the categories, the rating narrative will include these four letters: "BQAA." I wish I had a dollar for every time I have written those letters, which stand for "Better Qualified Applicants Available."

1. Personal impression

2. Communication skills

3. Enthusiasm

4. Leadership

5. Competence

6. Vocational maturity

7. Interest

Ten Surefire Ways to Make a PRO Grimace

1. Be shy and reticent with a lack of self-confidence.

2. Indicate that you are a "window shopper," a candidate

who already knows where he will probably work, but who just wants to check around in the job market.

3. Indicate that you aren't sure what you want to do.

4. Ask for career counseling in the interview.

5. Bring a copy of your senior class project for "show and tell" in the interview.

6. Have a nervous mannerism such as drumming your fingers on the desk or ending each statement with ". . . you know?"

7. Don't ask any challenging questions. Instead, say things like, "Boy, it really sounds good; I can't think of any questions."

8. Apologize because you didn't have time to read any literature on the company.

9. Knock on the interviewer's door to get him to hurry up with the evaluation he is trying to complete on the last candidate.

10. Answer a question with the trite and worthless statement, "I really like working with people."

Conclusion

The chances of getting an offer correlate with your knowledge of the recruiter's needs and requirements. As a closing caveat I offer a warning regarding the stereotyping of interviewers into any pigeonhole or category. *Each recruiter is a unique type unto himself.* Some YFTs wear wing tips and some TPs have a strong interest in leadership skills. The point of this chapter is that you must recognize each interviewer as a unique individual who will apply his company's requirements and his own personal biases in the selection process. Don't interview with a vague entity: interview with someone's next-door neighbor who drives a Chevy with a tilt steering wheel.

The Evaluation: Why You Can Be Witty, Friendly, Intelligent, and Outgoing and Still Get a Turndown

9.1 INTRODUCTION

All interviewees know that some kind of an evaluation will be written following the interview, and for most candidates, a foggy concept of the evaluation process and the rating form contributes to the excessive nervousness that is so often seen and negatively reacted to by interviewers. Unfortunately, many recruiters contribute to the anxiety problem by actually writing God knows what on a form during the actual interview. The convenient placement of a briefcase or the not so subtle art of positioning an arm to cover the form to seemingly protect its secrecy further leads the candidate to a feeling of apprehension and even uncomfortable fear regarding that piece of paper. I don't ever recall being asked the question, "What kind of personal attributes and qualifications does your company value?" or in plain talk, "What is on that form you are shielding behind the briefcase?" Quite the opposite; I have observed candidates consciously avoiding looking in the direction of the form as if it were an infringement on a hostile country's territorial waters.

Let's get rid of the arm, move the briefcase to the side, and closely examine the rating form and the evaluation process to eliminate or at least reduce the anxiety that can impinge on interviewing success.

9.2 NO ONE LIKES THE RATING FORM

For the interviewer, completion of the rating form is probably the least enjoyable part of the interviewing process because it is tedious, sometimes difficult, and almost always must be accomplished either between scheduled interviews (while the next candidate is knocking on the door) or at night in the Holiday Inn during commercial breaks on the late movie. If the recruiter doesn't exercise either of those unattractive options, the form gets completed two days later when it's a challenge just to remember the name of the candidate, much less the specific evaluatory factors. This should offer at least some consolation for the candidate who is being written about and interviewed at the same time because, whether positive or negative, the notes taken during an interview represent the most valid rating you could achieve with that recruiter. The impressions are being recorded as you speak and therefore, for whatever it's worth, they are the gut-level evaluations of the recruiter. Good luck if your form is being completed while the recruiter is sitting at the airport waiting for the red-eye flight back home.

The pressure on the interviewer to complete the form accurately is heightened by the fact that the form is both directly and indirectly the mechanism that generates his or her own performance rating and ultimately defines success or failure as a recruiter. In a sense, his job and your possible future job are both on the line as the recruiter hurriedly completes the evaluation. No one likes the rating form.

9.3 THE RATING FORM DESIGN

Rating forms vary widely among companies in length and format, but are generally standard as far as what is being rated.

Sample Rating Form (Figure 2)

APPLICANT PROFILE—AMERI-CAN COMPANY

INTERVIEWER:

APPLICANT NAME: DATE:

ADDRESS: LOCATION:

GRADUATION DATE: HOME PHONE:

COLLEGE: BUS. PHONE:

DEGREE(S):   G.P.A. (MAJOR):

GEOGRAPHIC   WHERE INTERVIEWED:
  PREFERENCE:

HOMETOWN: PERSONAL IMPRESSION:
                                             1 2 3 4

CITIZENSHIP: COMMUNICATION SKILLS:
                                             1 2 3 4

POSITION: LEADERSHIP: 1 2 3 4

COMMENTS: INTEREST: 1 2 3 4

                                             ENTHUSIASM: 1 2 3 4

                                             VOCATIONAL MATURITY:
                                             1 2 3 4

                                             COMPETENCE: 1 2 3 4

                                             OVERALL RATING: 1 2 3 4

ACTION RECOMMENDED: MAKE OFFER   SECOND INT.
                        TURN DOWN   REFERRAL

With the advent of inexpensive automation/computerization of records, most forms include a limited narrative accompanied by rating codes (for computer input) for each evaluation category. Computerizing interview evaluations allows companies to order system queries such as, "List all candidates with marketing majors, relevant work experience, an above average overall rating, and an outstanding rating in communication skills." The computer will then print a list of all candidates meeting the given parameters. This method of employee selection is certainly dehumanized and is often unfair, but such use of computerized screening is becoming the norm rather than the exception. *You simply must achieve good ratings in order for the computer to print out your file for human consideration*. (Figure 2 is an example of a typical rating form.)

After examining the rating form example, you may wonder why so much space is taken up by questions that almost certainly are answered by your resume or completed application. There are two reasons for the redundant capturing of data:

1. The rating form serves as the standard computer input tool for the keypuncher. The standardized form increases accuracy and efficiency.

2. Information must be again checked because of the dynamic nature of job seekers, who typically change addresses, names, and phone numbers almost as often as residents of Los Angeles. Capturing current information about job applicants is like trying to nail jello to a tree.

I recall interviewing a graduate who had submitted a resume that stated the following career objective: "I am seeking a challenging career opportunity in research and development or facility engineering." Since I was on campus to interview sales candidates I commented that his career objectives to get into research would not logically be facilitated by beginning a career in sales. (I have a tendency for understatement.) The Penn State Nittany Lion turned red, rifled through his folder, and as he handed me another resume apologized for presenting the "wrong" resume. His second resume indicated that the

only thing in life that interested him was working as a salesman. He had honestly done a 180-degree career turn in a matter of a few months. Either that or he was using the "if it's
Tuesday it must be sales" multiple-resume system.

Recruiters verify and double-check all standard information
such as degree, phone number, etc., because it is often subject
to change. Furthermore, the verification procedure itself leads
to discussion that may provide valuable evaluatory data and
information. In the Penn State example above, the candidate
was turned down due to his "vocational immaturity." *He really
didn't know what he wanted to do, a surefire death knell in any interview.*

9.4   THE HEART OF THE RATING

The following major evaluation categories are fairly standard. Examine the rating categories carefully because, in total,
they spell success or failure in every interview:

1.	**Personal Impression**	neatness, presence, busi-ness maturity, confidence, attitude, sociability, tact
2.	**Communication Skills**	logic, written and oral skills, conciseness, articu-late
3.	**Enthusiasm**	interest, sincerity
4.	**Leadership**	leadership potential
5.	**Competence**	knowledge in field, exper-tise, work experience, grades
6.	**Vocational Maturity**	clearly defined goals, knowledge of strengths and weaknesses, realistic self-concept

7. **Interest**   knowlege of company,
                                         well prepared for inter-
                                         view

The seven evaluatory categories are all subjective in nature and obviously reflect the difficulty anyone would have in rendering an accurate assessment based on a thirty-minute or one-hour conversation. The odds work against your ever receiving a truly accurate evaluation because the recruiter has to rely on instinct, bias, inference, and brief character glimpses that just scratch the surface of who you are. The good news for you is that few job seekers recognize the seven major categories and therefore plod along in the interview relying on luck, intelligence, and friendliness. You have a competitive edge.

Use the powerful interviewing tool (SETS) offered in Chapter 6, "How to Prove Your Way to a Job Offer," as the foundation to achieve an outstanding rating in each of the seven categories. Prior to each interview, you should plan to use specific SETS for various evaluation categories. Following are examples to illustrate why a candidate receives an outstanding rating in various categories as opposed to the 95 percent who will receive average or above average ratings.

1. Personal Impression
   a. Average rating: "Hello, Mr. Saylor. How are you today? It looks like it's going to rain."

   b. Outstanding rating: "Hello, Mr. Saylor. I'm really glad I was able to get this interview. You know we have a chance lottery system for interview sign-ups so I was really pleased when I learned that you pre-screened me in. I received a copy of your latest annual report and was really excited to learn about the recent purchasing department reorganization. The decentralized approach is really my cup of tea."

2. Communication Skills
   a. Average rating: "I really like working with my hands."

   b. Outstanding rating: "I know it sounds trite to say that I am a 'hands-on' person, but I really enjoy being on the shop floor because of the production, planning, and people challenges that present themselves simultaneously whether you ask for them or not. The excitement of making decisions without the luxury of a committee or a task force requires that you muster all available input and then direct an action plan. I really thrive on that kind of pressure. For example . . . (SET).

3. Enthusiasm

a.   Average rating: "I read your brochures and the management training program really sounds interesting. Could you tell me more about it?"

b.   Outstanding rating: "Your management training program really sounds interesting. The brochure explained that trainees are moved through various departments for six months so that you get exposed to many business activities and gain a broad understanding of the company. I think that is a great idea because it is so important to understand the overall direction of the company so that I can apply the same directon and impetus in specific tasks and functional goals. Did you go through the program yourself?"

4. Leadership

a.   Average rating: "I was captain of the hockey team and have always considered myself a leader."

b.   Outstanding rating: "Besides my being elected class president, which I feel is at least as much a leadership indicator as it is a popularity contest, I think the best example that addresses my leadership potential was . . . (SET to prove leadership).

5. Competence

a.   Average rating: "I have a 3.1 grade point average, which I feel accurately reflects my level of knowledge. As you know, this is a tough school."

b.   Outstanding rating: "I really had to work hard for the 3.1 G.P.A. because I participated in two sports and held down a part-time job. The G.P.A. carries significant weight, and speaks for itself, but I believe my drive and ambition to learn is equally as important. I will apply that same dedication and drive as I begin my career, and I expect to face a continual learning challenge throughout my life. My degree is an excellent foundation, but I know there is a lot more to learn and I am excited about it."

6. Vocational Maturity

a. Average rating: "I went into marketing because I really enjoyed the advertising brand management course I took as a freshman. I'm glad I chose this field. I am looking forward to applying the theory to the real world."

b. Outstanding rating: "I have always enjoyed the challenges of marketing. I first developed an interest as a paper boy when I won a trip to Norway as an award for top marketer. I developed a plan that identified a group of potential subscribers, and it worked. During high school I was chairman of our highly successful class fund drive for three years. Marketing has always been in my blood. In fact, I chose this school primarily because of its fine marketing program reputation."

7. Interest

a. Average rating: "I read your brochures and annual report. Sounds like a good company. Where is your headquarters?"

b. Outstanding rating: "I was very much interested to learn that you have thirty-five sales offices throughout the United States. I called up your local sales office in Pittsburgh and was fortunate to arrange an information interview with Mr. Tom Guss, the sales manager. He provided an excellent tour of the facility, and I was impressed with the people, atmosphere, and extensive training that is provided for new employees. After that visit I must say that your company is my number-one choice."

If you are one of the 95 percent who generally receive an average or above average rating you should be recoiling right now and thinking, "I can't say those things! I never was elected to anything! I can't go on an information interview with a company that is located 300 miles from my home! This whole approach sounds a little aggressive to me."

Recognize this fact: Your competition *was* elected to a leadership position, your competition *did* contact a local sales office and has *always* wanted a job in marketing since age twelve. You may be the best candidate for the job, but the recruiter has to take his best guess and run with it. *Best candidates do not receive offers, candidates who receive the best ratings do.* Whom would *you* select based strictly on the preceding example responses? Interviewers are merely professional gamblers who have been provided a thirty-minute tip sheet analysis to help decide on which candidate to place the bet.

9.5   NEVER UNDERESTIMATE YOUR COMPETITION

I once interviewed the number-two quarterback for a Big Ten university football team who happened to be the backup for a national college star. I asked him why he wasn't number one. He explained that he could pass effectively and accurately, but that the number-one national star was *just a little bit better.* Tiny fractions of seconds and inches were the difference between a national star and an unknown backup. That same concept and rule applies to the job search process. *The tiniest bit of extra effort that shows in an interview is often the only difference between an offer and a turndown letter.* I have probably not emphasized that sentence enough. FACT: Most candidates receive average or above average ratings, and that is simply not good enough to compete against the candidate who receives an outstanding rating.

9.6   THE RATING FORM NARRATIVE

The narrative or comment section on the rating form consists of the interviewer's subjective feelings and his notes regarding miscellaneous factors that affect the decision to make an offer or send a turndown. For example, if the recruiter really wants to make you an offer in spite of your low grades, he must document the logic and reason for exception. On the other hand, if you have straight A's and an M.B.A. and own 30 percent stock in the company, he'd better document the reason he has decided to send a turndown. Let's get to the real bottom line of the rating form narrative.

The narrative is the section on the rating form where the interviewer validates the "yes" or "no" decision that has already been made. If the interviewer has decided to give you an offer, he will write positive statements and comments to support his decision. I have reviewed thousands of rating forms and have never seen one—either positive or negative—in which the rating was not supported by the comment section. Strive toward receiving an outstanding rating in each of the seven evaluation categories in order to get an offer. The narrative will always follow suit.

Conclusion

The evaluation is a necessary pain in the neck for both you and the interviewer. It is your ticket to an offer or a turndown and the interviewer's ticket to a pay raise or a poor performance rating.

Your goal should be to receive an outstanding rating in each rating category. You know what is on the form now . . . so just go for it. Don't be fearful of the rating form, but rather be driven to help the recruiter complete the form by exhibiting the required traits. Don't make the mistake that so many candidates do by relying on the, "Gee, I'm a witty, friendly, intelligent, and outgoing person" strategy to land an offer. Prove to the recruiter that you should get an outstanding rating in each of the seven evaluation categories, and you will succeed in getting job offers.

10

The P's and Q's of
Job Search Letters

10.1   INTRODUCTION

Nothing is more important to a successful job campaign than
having absolutely outstanding written materials. Because you
will always be competing with job candidates who have qualifications as good as or better than yours, you must somehow
set yourself apart with a great looking application, resume, and
cover letter. You could be the perfect person for the job, but if
your credentials are poorly presented, they will go directly to the
garbage can or to a big file cabinet labeled "Resumes." In either
case the result is the same; your file will never again see the
light of day. The only reason companies have resume files is so
that they can say, "Yes, we did receive your letter. We have it
on file and you will be considered for any openings that match
your credentials." Under consideration? Balderdash! Once your
materials are filed the only thing they will be under is thousands of other files. If your materials don't make an outstanding impression in the ten to twenty seconds' review they will
receive, they're gone forever.

In this chapter we'll examine what it takes to *avoid* having
your materials placed in the file, and instead to generate a very
pleasant phone call to arrange an interview. The goal of this
chapter is not to offer letter examples that you can copy or steal
from, but rather to explain the logic behind various ap-

proaches that will facilitate your creating the best written materials for yourself.

Generally speaking, it is not the *format* that is the key to developing outstanding materials, but rather the *words* selected to describe your credentials. The concept of carefully selecting words is critically important. Consider this analogy: A classic poem may have only fifty words, yet somehow and for some reason has stood the test of time for centuries. It could be argued that each word in the poem is "perfect" for that poem's purpose. If, for example, the poet had chosen the wrong word, perhaps the poem would never have been remembered. A word that was not a perfect fit could have destroyed the "wholeness" of the poem.

Your written materials are not intended to become classic examples of great writing, but you must spend considerable time and effort in selecting the best words for your purpose. Since few of us are great writers or poets, you must seek out criticism of your letters. Remember, your letter will receive literally just a few seconds of review. This chapter's goal is to teach you how to maximize those few seconds.

10.2   PAPER AND LAYOUT

Your written materials are advertising brochures for a product that is very expensive to purchase. Even a clerk earning $12,000 per year multiplied by twenty years is a quarter-of-a-million-dollar investment! A professional person could easily cost a million dollars over a career. Don't attempt to market such an expensive product on cheap paper or twenty-cent Xerox copies.

Paper Weight.   Rag bond paper has cotton fiber along with wood pulp and looks and feels much sturdier and richer than paper made of wood pulp only. Don't use cheap paper purchased from your local multinational conglomerate. *Use rag bond paper and envelopes*. Never use flimsy, see-through paper that looks and feels cheap. Visit an office supply store and purchase a good-quality paper.

Color. Don't use pure white or unusual colors such as green, pink, blue, or yellow. *Use off-white, tans, beiges, or grays to achieve a professional, businesslike appearance.* Before selecting a paper color, make sure that you have correction fluid to match. A beige letter corrected with white correction fluid is completely unprofessional.

Typing. Your competitors for the job will be using word processors and professional typesetting to give their materials a professional look. If you don't have access to a word processor, at least use a good electric typewriter with a new ribbon to type your letters. Any letter key that strikes unclean or blurred spells disaster. Don't ever use a manual typewriter. A professional image is necessary because you *are* that piece of paper.

If you make a lot of typing errors, have someone else do your typing. Don't send letters coated with correction fluid.

Balance. Letters and resumes should be centered on the page with at least a three-quarter-inch margin on the sides and a one-inch margin top and bottom. If you can't center the letter, have someone else type it, but don't send a letter that is not perfectly centered. Is this picky? Yes it is. Is it important? You bet!

10.3   COVER LETTERS

Cover letters should first capture the attention of the reader, then stimulate or heighten interest, and then in closing generate some kind of action.

1. Capture attention

2. Stimulate interest

3. Generate action

The letter must be neat, accurately typed, and well organized and should rarely exceed one page. It is easy to be wordy.

Write concisely and to the point. Be brief. We will examine five kinds of cover letters:

1. Cover letters for answering job ads

2. Cover letters for contacting friends and acquaintances

3. Cover letters for contacting professional recruiters

4. Direct mail or unsolicited cover letters

5. Interview thank-you letters

10.4   COVER LETTERS FOR ANSWERING JOB ADS

First of all, whenever possible, send the letter to a specific person. Many ads have a blind box number or request that resumes and letters be sent to "Director, Human Resources" or to "Ajax Company, P.O. Box 10," for example. Place a high priority on sending letters to human beings as opposed to a post office box or a nameless personnel head. How excited are you when you get mail addressed "Occupant"? A letter addressed to a specific person has much more impact and power—remember that you are trying to somehow separate yourself from the masses.

If the ad requests that you send a letter to the director of human resources, phone the company and get the name of the individual. If the ad is a blind P.O. box, look for clues in the advertisement to try to figure out who is advertising, then get the name of the person who can hire you and send your letter directly and personally to him. For example, if the ad says, "Local growing building products company, division of Fortune 500 company, seeks experienced credit manager," a quick phone call to the chamber of commerce or a little bit of library research will help you figure out exactly which company is advertising the job opening. Knowing the company will allow you the added benefit of tailoring the letter to meet the needs of that specific company.

Another approach in answering job ads is to bypass the personnel office and send the response directly to the person who could hire you. For example, if the job ad is for a maintenance supervisor, send a letter directly to the V.P. of operations or the superintendent of maintenance. Call up the night watchman and ask him to look in the company phone book for the name of the individual you wish to write to. Whenever possible, send your materials to the person who can hire you. Personnel managers are only paper shufflers and "screener-outers." Personnel managers have the authority to send you a turndown, but rarely will have authority to send an offer. Avoid personnel people.

The first part of your letter should explain how you decided to respond to the ad. Your goal is to capture the reader's attention:

Dear Mr. Wulter,

Your recent ad in the <u>Tribune</u> emphasized the need for a candidate experienced in cost accounting backed up with solid communication skills. I offer a successful track record of accomplishments in cost accounting for a major manufacturer and consider communication ability with all levels of staff and operating levels my greatest strength.

Dear Ms. Evans,

Your advertisement in last Sunday's <u>Gazette</u> sounds like a perfect mesh with my goals and qualifications. You evidently recognize the importance of exceptional typing and shorthand skills for an executive secretary. I offer the speed and accuracy required, but furthermore have the creativity, professional presence, and aggressiveness to provide administrative support for the most demanding executive.

Dear Mr. Saylor,

Backed by seven years of successful experience in advertising/brand management, I am seeking a challenging position with a growth company. Your recent advertisement in the <u>Morning Sun</u> for a marketing manager called for experience in analysis and product management, an area in which I offer an unusual record of accomplishment.

After capturing the attention of the reader, your cover letter should stimulate interest by highlighting accomplishments that directly correspond to the company's needs. Use quantified results in terms of dollar savings, improved profit, etc., to add significance and weight to your accomplishments. Prove interest and professionalism by mentioning something that you found out about the company in your research. Personalizing the letter is worth the time and research required.

> ... Your Mr. Tom Kelly, regional sales manager, suggested that my management style and success in reducing variable costs might be of interest to you. As Operations Supervisor, I have improved productivity by 17 percent and designed and implemented a productivity gain sharing program that has morale and enthusiasm higher than it has ever been.

> ... Your annual report has emphasized your commitment to systems and automation, and I am experienced with the problems of implementing large-scale manufacturing systems very similar to your MJP system.

The closing of your letter should call for action.

> ... I have enclosed a resume that provides additional documentation of my accomplishments. I'll give your office a call next week to request an interview.

> ... I have enclosed a resume for your consideration and welcome the opportunity to discuss how I can contribute as marketing manager. In that regard, I'll be calling your office next week to see if we can set up a meeting to discuss your needs.

Summary

Your cover letter must accomplish three goals:

1. Get attention

2. Stimulate interest

3. Generate action

Cover Letter to Answer Advertisement

Ms. Sarah Boulder
201 Second Avenue
Mahomet, IL 64796
217-666-6547

September 25, 1986

Mr. William Grenter
Vice President, Human Resources
Ameri-Can Corporation
301 Gateway Plaza
Atlanta, GA 11303

Dear Mr. Grenter,

Your advertisement in last Sunday's <u>Chicago Tribune</u> for a
personnel trainee sounds like a perfect match with my own
credentials and goals. As highlighted in your ad and your
recent annual report, Ameri-Can is a leader in recognizing
human resources as a valuable asset that must be managed.
The track record of your company, particularly your recent
increase in market share, spells many challenges in human
resources. I believe I can contribute.

I offer a B.A. in Liberal Arts with a strong emphasis in psy-
chology and personnel administration. My greatest
strength is in communications, and I most recently was on
the university championship debate team. I am a fast
learner and a team player who can effectively implement
policies and procedures.

Enclosed is a resume which provides additional supporting
detail of my accomplishments. I will call your office next
week to request an interview meeting. Thank you for your
consideration.

Sincerely,

Sarah Boulder

10.5   COVER LETTERS TO PERSONAL CONTACTS

The unpublished job market is where 80 percent of the jobs are. Phone calls and letters to personal and business acquaintances provide excellent job leads:

Dear Mr. Herman:

You may recall that I lived next door to your family for one year prior to my leaving for Indiana University. The time has really gone by, and I will be graduating this spring with a degree in chemistry. I know that you were a chemist with Kraft Foods, and I was hoping that perhaps you might provide some employment leads for me.

I am actively interviewing on campus, but with your experience and contacts in the field, I would appreciate any guidance or ideas that you may have regarding employment.

I have enclosed a resume for your review and hope you don't mind if I give you a call next week. Thanks ahead of time for your help.

Dear Ms. Scott:

I was fortunate enough to work for Ameri-Can last summer, and you may recall that I was the employee who presented the paper on stress. The experience was extremely valuable because I learned that I am a hands-on engineer who would be extremely happy working in production management as opposed to design engineering.

I am graduating this spring with a B.S.M.E. from Georgia Tech., and I am writing to call on help from Ameri-Can once again. I was hoping that I might spend a few minutes with you next week to get some career guidance. I'll give your office a call on Friday to see if we could arrange a brief meeting. I have enclosed a resume for your review.

Please pass along my hello and thanks to Mr. John Carle. He was a great supervisor. Thank you for your assistance.

Dear Mr. Taylor:

I have lived in your district for fifteen years and have always admired your integrity and commitment to your constituency. My parents have actively worked in each of your campaigns, and it is on their advice that I am writing.

I am graduating with a liberal arts degree from Penn State and am seeking an entry-level management trainee position in business. With your vast knowledge of our community and familiarity with our business leaders, I was hoping that you might provide some guidance as to which employers may have need of a young, aggressive, and hardworking college graduate. I would appreciate any guidance or help that you may provide. I have enclosed several copies of my resume for your review and possible referral.

10.6 COVER LETTERS FOR CONTACTING EMPLOYMENT AGENCIES

Dear Ms. Bergman:

On the chance that you may have a client in need of an experienced salesman in pharmaceuticals, I have enclosed a resume for your consideration.

Until recently, I have been the Midwest Division Manager for Chemco Corporation, responsible for three million dollars in sales. A recent reorganization and consolidation placed my division under the broad umbrella of a new national sales group, and my position was eliminated. I declined an offer for a staff marketing position because of my commitment to sales management.

My track record is outstanding, including being named Manager of the Year last year, and my enclosed resume demonstrates recent accomplishments and expertise. If you should have any clients interested in such a background, I would be most pleased to enter into discussions with them.

Dear Mr. Kane:

I am a recent graduate of the University of Toledo interested in securing a position as management trainee. I would prefer a manufacturing environment that requires a hands-on supervisor with a well-rounded background in communications and management.

I have worked for Ameri-Can Corporation for the past three summers as a management intern in operations management and gained valuable experience as a temporary supervisor. Enclosed is a brief resume that highlights my credentials and experience. I will call your office next week to discuss a possible meeting. Thank you for your consideration.

10.7   INTERVIEW THANK-YOU LETTERS

Always send a thank-you letter immediately following an interview. *Always* include a personal note about your background to heighten company interest. *Always* be brief:

Dear Mr. McGill:

Thank you for the opportunity to discuss career possibilities with Ameri-Can. Since our meeting I have completed additional research on your company and in particular was excited about an article in <u>Business Week</u> (3/10) that praised your efforts in strategic planning.

I am convinced that the marketing assistant position is a great match with my own career goals, and my summer experience with Ajax will allow me to immediately begin contributing. I just received my final grades and am pleased to inform you that my G.P.A. went up to a final cumulative 3.4.

Please pass along my thanks to Ms. Mary Schelhouse; her enthusiasm and her pride in Ameri-Can are contagious. I'll be looking forward to hearing from you. Thanks again.

OR

Dear Ms. Kelley:

I enjoyed our interview last week and just wanted to drop a line thanking you and your staff for the fine hospitality. The efficiency and thoroughness of your interview format were appreciated.

The position of management trainee at your Rantoul restaurant sounds like a great match with my experience and career goals. As you know, I worked for three summers in a fast-food restaurant and thrived on the fast-paced pressure of meeting consumers' needs.

Relocating to Rantoul presents no problem on my part. The advantages of living near a major university are a real plus. As you can probably tell, I am very much excited about the opportunity and challenges that you presented, and I am looking forward to hearing from you. I appreciate your consideration. Thanks again for an important and good day.

10.8   UNSOLICITED LETTERS TO POTENTIAL EMPLOYERS

Direct mail to potential employers based on annual reports, contacts, newspaper articles, etc., is an excellent approach to the job search. Your competition is minimal because the opening has not been published. Careful research of business change indicators (see Chapter 3) will increase your ability to cash in on the hidden job market.

Following are two sample letters that will provide a rough framework for you to use. Use all of your creative juices to write a powerful letter. Get help from your spouse, friends, and counselor. Read the letter aloud. Once you write ten or fifteen direct mail letters, they will fall into a pattern, and you'll be able to easily send out five to ten letters each week. It is hard work, but it is the most important assignment you'll ever have.

Dear Mr. Coulter:

A few weeks ago I noted in the Sunday Gazette that you were promoted to manager of personnel for Ameri-Can Corporation. I would like to first offer my congratulations and then offer my resume in consideration for a position on your staff.

I am currently benefits administrator for Ohio Northern Railroad and most recently was responsible for designing and implementing a flexible benefit package for 5,000 employees. The package reduced our employment costs by $300,000 per year.

I am seeking to widen my exposure to other areas of human resources with the eventual goal of becoming a generalist. I would like to take the liberty of calling your office next week to arrange a brief meeting. I hope all is going well in your new position and I thank you for your consideration.

Dear Mr. Saston:

Your recent annual report states that you will be modernizing and subsequently doubling the capacity of your Dallas plant by the end of next year. Technological change and expansion always create special management challenges and in that regard I am writing to offer my resume in consideration for a position in project management or operations management.

I am currently an operations supervisor for Wiley & Sons, a medium-sized foundry in Minnesota. I most recently managed a ten-million-dollar capital project that came on line thirty days early and $450,000 under budget. My major strength is in controlling costs and implementing projects on time.

I often visit Dallas because my in-laws live in a northern suburb, and I really enjoy the climate and business environment. Relocation would present no problem. I will call your office next week to discuss my background in greater detail. Thank you for your consideration.

Conclusion

A great cover letter is critical to job search success. Spend a considerable amount of effort in choosing the best words to suit your purpose. The amount of effort expended on your cover letters will be directly proportional to your success ratio in receiving interviews. Following are ten points to remember:

1. Three parts: Capture attention, Stimulate interest, Generate action.

2. *Always send letters to a human being whenever humanly possible*. Avoid "Dear Personnel Head." Don't send form letters unless you are using a word processor to give the appearance of an original personal letter.

3. *Proofread* each letter for content by reading it slowly aloud, then read each word starting with the last word in the letter to check for spelling errors. One spelling error is a professional disaster.

4. *Be creative and brief.* Don't be cute.

5. *Highlight your quantifiable accomplishments* that directly fit the job.

6. *Use quality rag bond paper.*

7. *Use only an electric typewriter or word processor.*

8. *Get accurate titles and spellings of names.*

9. *Invest a lot of thought in creating a powerful letter.*

10. *Write in first person.* Use "I," not "he." A third-person approach sounds schizophrenic.

Nothing is more important than your written materials. Without outstanding letters you will not be successful. Remember, it is not the best candidate who gets the job, but rather the person who is best *at* getting the job.

11

Resumes:
A Fifteen-Second Interview

11.1 INTRODUCTION

Companies receive millions of resumes each year. One typical Fortune 500 company receives more than eight thousand unsolicited resumes annually. A newspaper advertisement can generate hundreds of responses. It should come as no surprise, then, that your resume will generally receive only a cursory five- to twenty-second review. Don't picture an executive or personnel manager sipping a cup of coffee and leisurely strolling through your resume:

> "Oh, he enjoys chess and gardening . . . so do I. I see he was captain of his hockey team . . . hmmmmm. And look here, he has two little girls, isn't that nice."

No way! Reviewing resumes is a 78 rpm process, not 33⅓. Reviewers scan resumes in seconds, searching for reasons to trash them. A resume is the primary tool utilized to generate turndowns. If, for example, a job requires four years' experience and you list at the top of your resume that you offer two years' experience . . . it's gone and the reviewer's eyes never even made it to the center of the page.

Quite simply, you must develop a resume that will not provide ammunition for a quick turndown. If the reviewer cannot immediately find a reason to trash the file, it will advance to a smaller stack on the desk and receive a more thorough review later. The goal of a resume is twofold:

1. To avoid getting trashed in the first five to fifteen seconds.

2. To generate an interest level that warrants a phone call or written invitation to interview.

After a resume serves its purpose of helping land the interview, its value diminishes. It becomes a scratch pad to jot down notes about you, or perhaps will be used as a tool to generate questions in the interview. The job selection process leaves the level of written words and goes to an encounter of the human kind. After human contact is made, the employment decision process will hinge on your interviewing skills. An outstanding resume is a ticket to an interview.

11.2   BASIC RESUME FORMATS

A resume has six basic informational sections. Each section has a specific purpose and must be carefully executed to maximize the effectiveness of the resume. *The resume is only as strong as its weakest section:*

Section I: Name and Address
Section II: Objective statement
Section III: Experience/accomplishments
Section IV: Education/training
Section V: Special awards/achievements
Section VI: Personal

The format of a resume refers to the placement order of the sections within the resume and the approach taken in presenting each section. Most job seekers should use the six sections shown and place them in the order listed. The guideline in selecting the order that you use is to place the sections in order of strength or importance.

For example, a young college graduate with minimal work experience should place education in slot three, followed by experience and accomplishments. For this candidate, education is stronger than experience and therefore should be presented first. A mature job seeker without a college degree should put training and special education at the tail end of the resume, in front of the personal section. For goodness' sake, don't use the first section of your resume to tell the reviewer about your height and weight—unless you're applying for a position as a jockey.

There is room for quite a bit of flexibility in how you present each section, but my strong recommendation is that you be more concerned about the individual words you select than about presentation style. Each section must be filled with the best words possible. It is not an easy task. If you complete your resume in two evenings, it's not nearly as strong as it could be. Each word must be carefully chosen to sell you. We'll take a close look at each section.

Resume Length

Develop a one- or a two-page resume. A one-and-a-half-page resume gives the impression that your entire life's experiences can't even fill two pages, and a three-page resume is simply unacceptably long. One full page or two full pages—no more, no less.

11.3 NAME AND ADDRESS

List first name, middle initial, and last name. Don't use Mr., Ms., Mrs., Esquire, or Dr. Many women of the eighties have chosen to keep their maiden names as kind of a middle name. Such a name is a progressive notion and it makes a statement about the individual that may be a strength or a liability depending on the company and position. Phone number should always include area code. Avoid limiting the times of day that you can be reached. Most companies will wish to contact you Monday through Friday, between 8:00 A.M. and 6:00 P.M. College students living on campus should consider using a parent's or friend's phone in lieu of a public telephone on the third floor of Animal House. If others will be answering the phone in your absence, be sure to teach them how to handle incoming phone calls from potential employers. Excellent manners and professionalism are required. Your eight-year-old daughter should say:

"My dad is not home right now, but may I take your name and number and have him return your call later today? I'll make sure he gets the message. Thank you for calling."

Frat brothers and sisters should band together. I wish I had a nickel for every time I heard this response:

"Yeah! I haven't seen him around today. Hey, Danny have you seen Bill? No, Danny ain't seen Bill either. He's probably in class. Hang on. I'll go find a pencil so I can take a message."

Depending on the length of your name and address, lay it out in a pleasant, crisp format that is pleasing to the eye:

Example:

Sylvia S. Hagstrom
6 Hardtop Road
Manchestor, TN 09647
618/416-6676

Example:

WILLIAM P. JONES

4785 16th Ave., Dallas, TX 76509, 315/599-6789

11.4   OBJECTIVE STATEMENT

The objective statement must be specific, yet as general as possible in order to avoid turndowns. Consider including a two- or three-sentence summary as part of the objective. Avoid trite, selfish expressions such as, "I am seeking a challenging position in which I can utilize my skills . . . ." Emphasize what you can do for the company. Don't list *your* requirements, sell what you offer. Following are a few examples to stimulate your own ideas:

Objective example:

HUMAN RESOURCES MANAGEMENT

Personnel specialist position in which creative problem-solving and highly developed interpersonal skills are required.

Objective example:

MARKETING SPECIALIST

Entry-level position requiring solid academic credentials, marketing experience, statistical analysis expertise, and an ability to work as a team player.

Objective example:

PRODUCTION MANAGEMENT

Where strong communication skills, leadership, and a proven record of results in a manufacturing environment are required.

Objective example:

ENGINEERING MANAGEMENT

Entry-level engineering management position that requires a solid technical base and broad business exposure.

Objective example:

MANAGEMENT TRAINEE

Where a well-rounded liberal arts background combined with resourcefulness, creativity, and initiative is required.

The objective must be general enough to include a broad functional area, yet specific enough to convince the reviewer that you know what you want. The following examples should help get you on track for this difficult and important task:

If you are seeking A, then your objective should be B.

A	B
Personnel trainee	Human resources management
Advertising trainee	Marketing management
Design engineering	Technical project management
Financial analyst	Accounting and finance administration
Television producer	Communications specialist
Retail trainee	Management assistant
Foreman	Supervisory management

Give your objective a lot of thought.

11.5 EXPERIENCE/ACCOMPLISHMENTS

Here's the real heart of the resume. Unless you have big gaps in your work history, such as three years of unemployment because you couldn't find a job, use a chronological presentation of your experience beginning with most recent experience. Recent experience should be emphasized with more detail than prior accomplishments. Accomplishments dating back ten years or more are of minimal value and interest to the reviewer. *Use short powerful action verbs to highlight accomplishments, not duties or responsibilities.* Never say, "I was responsible for. . . ." Make your resume come alive with an action verb followed by a noun. Quantify your accomplishments whenever possible.

Don't develop a resume that reads like an obituary notice:

NO:

> Production Clerk, American Corp., 3-78 to present. Responsible for billing, expediting, and administrative functions. Interfaced with purchasing department for inventory control matters.

YES:

> PRODUCTION ASSISTANT, American Corp., 3-78 to present. Cut inventory by 15%; Completed daily statistical analysis of scrap for General Manager; Developed monthly reports that fed 10 computer systems; Implemented new procedures that reduced order lead time by 25% ($50,000/year savings).

The first example describes a reactive paper shuffler. The person in the second example sounds alive and energetic. He probably runs to the bathroom so he can get back to the job quickly. Keep in mind that the two preceding examples describe the same job and the same person. Which one would you hire?

NO:

> Checker, K-Mart, 4-84 to present. Worked as a checkout girl, handled cash register and money record keeping.

YES:

> CUSTOMER SERVICE REPRESENTATIVE, K-Mart Corporation, Indianapolis, IN, 4-84 to present. Effectively handled 500 business transactions per day; Managed computerized check-out station—$5000/day. Perfect attendance award, conducted inventories, installed promotional displays. Known by supervisor as "innovative and dependable employee."

NO:

> Lifeguard, Cape May Beach, summers '84 and '85. Registered lifesaver/Red Cross.

YES:

> LIFEGUARD/BEACH MANAGEMENT, Cape May Department of Recreation, summer '84 and '85. Trained new lifeguards and administered Red Cross testing program, supervised five employees, ordered park equipment, scheduled work crews. Received Special Achievement Award.

Use action verbs to highlight accomplishments that will support your job search goals:

organized	created
established	eliminated
implemented	expanded
reduced	improved
saved	effected
streamlined	recommended
developed	finished
initiated	expedited
completed	trained

11.6 EDUCATION

Keep it brief. Don't spell out degrees; just list "B.S.," "B.A.," etc. Don't list the full address of the school, just the city and state. If the school is fairly well known, don't even bother with city and state. If you have a high G.P.A., (B− and above) list it. Don't ever list only the G.P.A. in your major area because that implies that you did poorly overall. If you graduated from a branch of a major university, just list the name of the mother school. Include any scholarships or special accolades. High school should never be mentioned if you have a college degree. Don't waste a lot of resume space in this section. Just lay the information down and get out. Following are some examples:

EDUCATION

Purdue University   B.S. Business Management 1985   G.P.A.
5.2/6.0 (graduated cum laude)

EDUCATION
University of Maryland   B.S. Mechanical Engineering   1984
Project Management Control   Management Institute   1983

11.7 SPECIAL AWARDS/AFFILIATIONS

Special achievements and leadership positions in community and school groups are interview-generating information. Membership in professional associations indicates an aggressiveness and desire to improve. Boy Scouts, PTA, PTO, Meals-on-Wheels, church groups, and volunteer charity organizations are examples of activities that may directly support your career goal. The information could be included in the experience section or highlighted in a section unto itself.

11.8 PERSONAL/HOBBIES

Don't ever list personal information at the top of the resume. Don't include personal information unless it enhances your chances of getting an interview.

For example, if you are single and are applying for positions in other states, make sure that you list marital status on your resume because it is cheaper and easier for a company to relocate a single job candidate.

Don't list height and weight unless the information will move you toward an interview invitation. It's pretty worthless information in most instances.

Only list your age if it is a strength for the position being sought.

Don't list your wife's name or other such "who cares" information as number of children. Do you buy a candy bar because Mr. Hershey has three grandchildren? You are a product, and unless you believe it is important to show that you are a family man or woman, forget the family tree mumbo-jumbo.

Hobbies
List hobbies or interests that fit the position you are applying for. Use this section to suggest that you are a well-rounded, "together" kind of candidate.

Conclusion

A resume is a ticket to an interview. Each word on the resume should be moving you toward that end. Don't waste any
words. Don't put "Resume" or "Biographical Sketch" on the top
of your resume. Even the dumbest reviewer will be able to figure out it's a resume without any help from you. Powerful action verbs are required. Spend many hours developing your
resume.

Read Richard Lathrop's book *Who's Hiring Who* (see Recommended Reading, page 181). Without a doubt it is the classic text on resumes.

12

Career Changers, Liberal Arts Graduates, and Other Problem Children

12.1 INTRODUCTION

In the fairyland of career development, an individual works his way through school, lands a great entry-level job in his field, gets promoted through the ranks, gets stymied for a promotional opportunity, and then goes job hunting for a higher-paying job. Everything fits according to the stereotypical American dream.

Back in the real world, many of us have a much more interesting (for lack of a better word) career path. Unlike Johnny American, we go to school for finance, graduate with nice grades, and then realize that we hate finance. Others try teaching for a while, get burned out with Huck Finn or simply decide to take a pass on poverty by getting a "real" job. Many go to school and get a liberal arts degree or general business degree that qualifies them to do everything and nothing at the same time.

This chapter is for all of us normal folks who quit school, changed majors, went into a field we didn't like, or otherwise have a career path that raises the eyebrows of the interviewer: In Chapter 7 we showed you how to positively handle liabilities in an interview. You will also face some special problems if you fall into any of the following categories:

Career changers   Liberal arts graduates
General business graduates   Housewives re-entering
Military personnel   labor market
                                   Seekers of part-time jobs

12.2   LIBERAL ARTS VERSUS INDUSTRY

Liberal arts graduates are hidden inside corporate America in great numbers. If you could examine the personnel records of a typical Fortune 500 company, you would probably become more excited about your job search prospects because you would find liberal arts people in all levels of the organization. Without a doubt, the most valuable talent to a company is the ability to communicate and get along with people. That talent is found in many liberal arts grads. A person can be trained to plug data into a formula to calculate wages, but can't be trained to be a sensitive and understanding communicator. The teaching profession is a great source of logical thinkers and great communicators. Liberal arts people know how to listen, a rare and critically important strength. Liberal arts graduates and teachers have much to offer industry:

1.   Communication skills: ability to work with all levels of management, sensitivity, empathy, diplomacy.

2.   Planning and organizational skills: ability to plan, organize, and implement programs.

3.   Lateral thinking: Engineers attack problems with a vertical step-by-step approach. Liberal arts people are more likely to see a solution out in right field. Industry needs creative thinkers who can turn problems upside down and think of radically different approaches to solve them. Competing in a world economy requires much more than a traditional approach to problem solving.

4.   Creativity: A liberal arts curriculum fosters creativity to a much greater extent than typical technical curricula.

5. Leadership skills: Teaching is a great leadership training profession. Motivating, directing, supervising, and counseling 150 eighth-graders is much more difficult than supervising a production line. Furthermore, teachers get the job done without support from government, parents, students, and the general public.

6. Loyalty and dedication: Teachers are committed and dedicated to a challenge. Idealism and dedication are valuable traits in the job market.

OK, that all sounds fine and good. Why then do teachers and liberal arts grads have so much difficulty landing good, high-paying jobs?

The problem with teachers and liberal arts grads is that they look, talk, and act like liberal arts graduates. To be successful in the job search, you must shed the image.

American industry does not like to admit that teachers and liberal arts grads are valuable. Many large companies will only interview technical graduates and will treat a young business graduate as a second-class citizen. You don't have to read the newspapers to know that everyone is on a technology bandwagon. Good companies know that people, not technology, are the secret to growth and success. Companies cannot buy their way to success, but rather must manage their way. Strange as it may sound, companies need you but don't want to admit it. Required on your part is a job search strategy that recognizes the biases afforded to all those without technical degrees.

You must enter the job market as a businessperson who just happens to have a liberal arts or non-technical background, not as a teacher or liberal arts grad who is seeking to land a job in business. Here's how:

To the extent that you can, disassociate specific references to your non-business background and training. For example, your resume should never list a "B.S. in Secondary Education"; instead, list "B.S." followed by your major area of study, e.g. Science, Marketing, Industrial Arts, Accounting, Mathematics, etc. A Bachelor of Science degree in Science conjures up a powerful image of a chemist or scientist—a technical person often required by industry. A Bachelor of Science in Education with a major in Science conjures up an image of a bespectacled nerd who did a poor job teaching Earth Science 101 for a bunch of little kids. A B.S. in English has a much more positive connotation than a B.S. in Education. A company is interested in hiring candidates with a special proficiency in English and communications, but has absolutely no interest in hiring an English teacher with suede patches on his jacket.

Candidates with degrees in elementary education should simply state: B.S., Education. Avoid alluding to the fact that you taught at the primary level. There is another bias that teaching kindergarten to sixth grade is merely experience as a glorified baby-sitter. The other stereotype that gets in the way is that of a young bride who taught kindergarten to pay for the family Winnebago. Avoid mentioning that you taught in primary grades.

These biases and prejudices should really make you angry! They reflect ignorance and are totally unfair. As a former high school teacher married to an elementary teacher, I know the value and importance of liberal arts and teaching. But you are not going to be interviewed by me. You will be interviewed by the businessperson on the school board who doesn't understand why teachers should be paid above the poverty line. There are strong biases against liberal arts graduates and teachers. They must be recognized in your overall job search strategy.

What the Business World Views as Weird Degrees

If you have a B.A. in something like anthropology or political science, sell yourself as a B.A., Liberal Arts unless the "weird" degree is directly applicable to the position sought. A B.A. in Political Science is "someone who always thought he wanted to go into law, but couldn't cut the mustard." A B.A. in Anthropology is so unusual that the company computer will not even recognize it as a legitimate degree. Use B.A., Liberal

Arts and then use supporting terminology to emphasize accomplishments that are meaningful for the career you seek.

Speak and write in business jargon:

(Elementary teacher at work)	"See the dragon. Look. Look. Hurry Jack. Press the return button."
(Elementary teacher in job interview)	"I developed and implemented a computer training program for more than five hundred students. From the initial proposal for funding to vendor selection and implementation, I worked closely with the school administrators. The project was completed on schedule and 10 percent under budget."

Use business terminology to describe your experience:

—You weren't a "class sponsor," you were "responsible for supervising and directing special projects for 480 students."

—You weren't on a "book selection committee," you "chaired a project team to evaluate and review educational curricula."

In your resume, letters, and interviews, present yourself as a businessperson. Use your creativity to avoid and overcome the liberal arts stereotypes. For the purposes of the job search, you didn't teach at Griffith High School, you taught for the Griffith School Corporation.

Look like a businessperson: Follow the guidelines for dress outlines in Chapter 4. Teaching attire and business dress are similar, but there are marked differences.

Invest considerable effort in research: Plan on investing extensive time in company and industry research to compensate for your non-business background.

12.3 B.S. MANAGEMENT/BUSINESS

If your degree is a B.S. in Management or Business, your marketability is only a notch or two above that of a liberal arts grad. The problem with a B.S. in Business is that you have had a little bit of exposure to all areas of business without the specialization required to effectively compete for a job in a specialized functional area.

A general degree in business is great for a career in retail management because a generalist background is beneficial. A retail management trainee will immediately get involved with inventory management, supervision, budgeting, etc. *Unfortunately, most entry-level jobs are specialized in nature.* What this means is that you will be competing against accounting, marketing, purchasing, and advertising majors for trainee positions open in those respective fields. It's one thing for a business graduate to say, "I could work in human resources because I have such a well-rounded background," and it is another to compete against a candidate who has forty-five credit hours in personnel administration.

You should avoid a shotgun job strategy approach and instead market yourself as a specialist in one or two broad areas. For example, if you want to work in marketing, highlight accomplishments that would support that specialized career goal. Use several different resumes geared to support your areas of expertise.

The greatest mistake made by business majors is not recognizing that the competitors for the position will have had specialized training.

Doomed approach: "I have a degree in business and am interested in working in purchasing, accounting, or personnel."

Better: "I offer a degree in business with a heavy emphasis in personnel administration. I am seeking a position in human resources."

If the company does not have an opening in personnel, let *them* suggest purchasing or supervision. You do not want to be the one to say, "Well, gee, if you don't have any openings in personnel, how about purchasing?" Such an approach is certain failure.

12.4   HOUSEWIVES

A housewife is experienced as an accountant, supervisor, counselor, business partner, community activist, purchasing director—and the list goes on. Unfortunately, like teachers, housewives are not generally recognized for their importance, value, and business skills.

It is the job of the housewife to sell her domestic experience as valuable business expertise. For example, teaching Sunday school might be described as follows:

4-80 to present: Sunday school administrator and teacher, ordered supplies, managed inventory, developed and implemented curriculum, trained new teachers, and implemented an expanded Sunday school schedule to meet increased demand. Attendance increased 30 percent in three years.

Community activities such as PTA, Girl Scouts, and Meals-on-Wheels are valuable experiences that serve to prove business and management skills and also present a positive image of an aggressive and active individual. It is important to tear down the image of the housewife as a "Mary Hartman" whose biggest concern for the day is deciding which brand of floor wax to purchase.

Of concern to recruiters is that the housewife is naive in business and has been sheltered from the pragmatic world of profit and loss. Housewives must convince the interviewer that they are quick to adapt, are in tune with current events, and will easily move into the labor market. Don't take the approach of a housewife who recently sent me a letter that said, "I am anxious to get in contact with the real world again."

Housewife to Businessperson

1. Get involved in community activities. Volunteer to take a leadership role for PTA, fundraising, religious committees, etc.

2. Communicate experience in business terminology.

3. Purchase a high-quality business suit. Forget that outfit buried in the back of your closet.

4. Seek professional help to develop an outstanding resume and letters. Ask a friend, your minister, or a local community college placement official to help. Don't attempt to do it all on your own.

5. Project yourself as a businessperson. Be poised and confident. Don't indicate fear or apprehension about returning to the labor force.

12.5 MILITARY PERSONNEL

Working to the advantage of veterans and retired military personnel is our nation's rekindled patriotism. Protests, Viet Nam, and Nixon have been replaced by a volunteer army, Grenada, and Reagan. Military people are again the symbol of the strength and pride of our country. The fact that you were in the military will not be as severe a liability as it would have been just a few years ago. Enjoy that good news, but you still have big problems.

The biggest liability facing you as a military retiree is the employer's fear that you won't adapt or fit into the corporate environment. You are leaving what is perceived to be an autocratic, non-participative environment that does not value individual innovativeness and creativity. American industry, on the other hand, is in the middle of a participative management revolution which recognizes that the lowest man in rank is often the best source for ideas on improving profit. Your experience in the military world runs head-on against America's new management style.

Another liability is your perceived lack of concern with profit and loss. The media is constantly telling the general public about how the military willingly pays hundreds of dollars for forty-nine-cent screws.

Your new mission is to land a job, and your job search strategy must recognize and then neutralize the biases and concerns.

Military Retirees

1. Get rid of the whitewalls and crewcut. It is much easier to assimilate into a new culture if you don't look like an outsider.

2. Don't use even one military abbreviation in your written materials. Use standard English. Your letters should be dated "May 12, 1986," not "12 May 86." Describe your training courses in descriptive English, not in "militarese."

3. Consolidate your experience into a two-page resume. Sure, you've had thirty-five assignments in eighteen different countries, but they must be encapsulated. Highlight your accomplishments for the last ten years.

4. Prove that you are oriented toward improving profits. Use examples from your past experience, and quantify results in dollar savings, reduced costs, etc.

5. Prove that you are participative in nature and welcome ideas and challenges from subordinates. You must convince the recruiter that you are not a tyrant from the "old military school."

Young Veterans

Recently discharged young veterans face the same liabilities as retirees, but to a much less severe degree. Present your military experience as if it were a job that you had for a few years. Highlight the valuable experience and training that directly support your capability to contribute to a company's bottom line. Use descriptive English—no military abbreviations.

12.6   CAREER CHANGERS

Career changers must always present themselves as being in complete control of their career development. Don't ever describe a career change as due to an external factor outside your control. Companies only hire candidates who are in control of their own destinies.

If, for example, you completed a degree in finance, but then discovered that you hate finance, don't present the experience as negative or as a mistake. Instead, say, "Even though I have a degree in finance, I have found that my real strength is in motivating and supervising people. Without a doubt, the finance background enhances my ability to manage inventory, develop budgets, and control costs, but I believe I can contribute most as a production supervisor. For example. . . ."

Think about the needs of the employer and the concerns that he may have regarding your background. Recognize your liabilities and handle them with the three-step procedure outlined in Chapter 7. Prove that you can meet the needs by using SETS (see Chapter 6).

12.7   HINTS FOR LANDING SUMMER OR
PART-TIME EMPLOYMENT

Temporary employees are often required to meet short-term narrowly defined business needs. For example, a summer job with the parks department might consist of cutting grass, or a retail store might have need of a stockperson to work over the holidays or of a temporary salesclerk for weekend evenings. Most temporary jobs require little training, and almost anyone could do the job. How then can a person get a competitive edge in landing a summer or temporary job?

To land a summer job you must determine the most important basic needs of the employer and prove that you meet those needs. Consider this example:

A fast-food restaurant manager has a need for a service clerk. Analyze his needs: the clerk must be

1. friendly, courteous, personable

2. fast

3. dependable

Prove that you can meet those needs and you'll get the job. He doesn't have time to interview extensively: he'll hire you. If you do not convince him that you meet all three needs, you'll lose out. Would a shy high school student get this job? No. Would a candidate who ambles in to the manager's office get the job? No. Concentrate on proving that you can meet the basic needs.

A good strategy for landing a temporary job is to make cold calls. Just walk into any store and ask to see the manager. Avoid the personnel director; go directly to the person who could hire you. If you want to work at a gas station, talk to the owner— not to the assistant manager. Seek out businesses that are seasonal: candy stores at Easter, retail stores at Christmas, and construction companies in the summer.

The most important tip is to determine the manager's needs and then prove that you can handle them.

Conclusion

Normal folks with a "screwy" career history have to work a little harder to prove that they offer a good return on investment. It is a little risky to hire a housewife as an administrative assistant. If your job strategy does not recognize the liabilities associated with your background, you will surely fail. On the other hand, if you identify the needs, prove that you can succeed, and handle the liabilities effectively, you will find yourself a career challenge. *You can do it.*

How to Get Promoted

13.1 INTRODUCTION

Have you ever wondered how and why certain individuals seem to move up quickly in their careers, receiving one promotion after another? Each of us probably knows someone who just shot right up the corporate ladder. What are the factors in such an ascension to power, authority, and high pay? While reading the business section of the newspaper, have you ever been curious about how young people are promoted to key positions such as general manager, vice-president, or director? Are they all brilliant, geniuses, relatives of company owners, or what? This chapter answers those questions and explains how to establish yourself in a new job and become recognized as an employee who should be groomed for a key management position. In simpler terms, this chapter teaches how to get promoted. The prescription outlined will work for employees in all levels and types of employment.

13.2 THE FANTASY OF CAREER DEVELOPMENT

To be successful in college, one must simply follow the directed curriculum format outlined in the school bulletin. A clear path to matriculation is charted, down to the finite level of which courses to take and when to take them. Very little decisive action is required on the part of the student. Constant feedback and reinforcement through tests and counseling sessions provides a continual, up-to-date status of progress. Housing, food, and even entertainment are included in the college plan. It is fair to say that most college students live in a pleasant, closed society, sheltered from the "real" world by the institution. I know there are some exceptions. New Jersey Tech is certainly not Walden Pond, and Case Western is separated from the real world only by fences and university security, but generally speaking, college life is not real world stuff. In most cases, you came to campus, you saw . . . and then someone told you which line to stand in.

With graduation come a diploma and a formal release from the protective custody of your alma mater. *Many graduates mistakenly assume that the new employer inherits the "protective custody" role by nurturing, guiding, and delineating a clear path to success.* New employees often expect the employer to provide explicit directions. Recruiters help foster this unfortunate illusion by speaking of grandiose training programs, management development programs, and performance appraisals, which all imply that someone will be watching out for you and plotting your career path. "Poppycock" is the nicest comment I can offer on this illusion.

Training programs are often nothing more than rotational on-the-job work experiences. Rarely will the training be as comprehensive or as formally structured as you expected. Companies are interested in beginning to reap the return on their investment (you) as quickly as possible. Don't count on company training programs to lead you to career success.

Although some companies conduct performance appraisals twice a year, most have only an annual review. Just once each year you will sit down with your supervisor for maybe an hour or so to discuss your accomplishments and areas requiring improvement. Good performance appraisal systems are few and far between. Business is still catching up with the science of evaluation, development of career paths, and positive reinforcement—and it has a long way to go. The performance appraisal process is often viewed by lower and even middle management as "another pain-in-the-neck corporate program" that carries a low priority. Another negative factor about the process is the tremendous variance in appraisers' ratings, due to personal biases. For example, one supervisor may believe that *all* of his employees are outstanding and will rate them accordingly, while another reserves an outstanding rating only for God and Lee Iacocca—your rating relies on the luck of the draw. To be promoted you need much more working for you than a performance appraisal. I am obligated to burst one more bubble regarding management development departments, and then we'll move on to positive actions you can take to control your career.

Management development departments exist in many large firms to perform the functions of manpower planning, succession planning, education and training administration, and sometimes counseling. Each company establishes the business priorities of these functions, and with the exceptions of manpower and succession planning, the functions are often considered less important than other activities that more directly affect production. To reduce employment costs, for example, a management development assistant position would most likely be eliminated before eliminating a direct production position such as assistant foreman. High-profit and growth companies are more likely to have excellent management development departments because they can afford them. Ironically, companies that need strong development programs (those that are losing money and have morale problems, for example) often eliminate or reduce management development functions in order to reduce fixed costs. Don't expect a management development coordinator to pull career development strings for you. You can't count on anyone but yourself to plot your career path or control your future.

There are a few companies that are noted for their fine career development programs, but without a doubt, the level of feedback, reinforcement, and guidance will drop significantly in the transition from college to business. *You must be prepared to implement actions that will place you in control of your own career growth.*

13.3   PERSONAL INTEGRITY

Personal integrity consists of honesty, high ethical and moral standards, and a value system that reflects respect for others. Integrity plays a major role in business success or failure. Without a doubt, a few cheats, liars, and amoral individuals attain power by using people and companies for personal gain. Television has glamorized such self-centered corporate leaders as national heroes. Forget J. R. Ewing and instead use Iacocca as your role model. Climbing a corporate ladder can be turned into a corrupt political game just like the TV shows, but integrity is a most powerful factor in achieving success. The workplace is a political arena only if you join in. Avoid the complications of political pandering. A reputation of impeccable integrity will carry you much farther than brownnosing or directing your career plan as if it were a political campaign. Let your supervisor know that you will never insult him by being a yes-man and that you'll never compromise your own integrity. Your supervisor needs to know that he can trust you and that your loyalty to help achieve prescribed goals will never be compromised. Serving your supervisor with integrity will carry you farther in your career than any political pandering.

13.4   DEVELOP PROFESSIONAL CREDIBILITY

A new employee's credibility rating is established within six months of employment. Credibility plays an important role in getting promoted and is based on three factors:

1.   Completing tasks on schedule

2.   Following through on all commitments

3.   Competence acknowledged by peers and supervisors

Strive to complete each assigned task on schedule or even prior to the deadline. Even if the job is relatively unimportant, get it done on time. *As soon as possible in your career you should strive to be labeled "results-oriented."* There is no excuse column when computing the bottom line of profitability. Become recognized as someone who can be counted on to get the job done.

Following through on commitments is much more important than most employees realize. If, for example, you tell a co-worker that you'll provide supporting documentation for his project by next week, make sure you do it.

It is critically important to gain a reputation as someone who follows through with commitments and who is dependable. Seemingly unimportant commitments are easily shelved as higher-priority tasks come into play. Honor all of your commitments. A common method of managing commitments is to list each one on a sheet of paper that permanently resides on your desk as a constant memory jogger. As a phone call is returned or a task completed, the item gets crossed off the list. *If you want to get promoted, consciously strive to honor all of your commitments.*

To be recognized for competence you must always get the facts and think before speaking. It does not speak well to offer to the project team a wonderful new idea that was already tried and ruled out as a viable solution two years ago. Do your homework. Instead of spewing out your opinions and ideas, analyze and study the problem thoroughly before offering input. Good ideas win professional respect from peers and supervisors. *Quantity of input should be reduced to quality of input.* Your goal is to have such a reputation of professional competence that when you speak, people listen. Fast-trackers offer plans, suggestions, and input that help achieve prescribed goals.

Professional credibility and contributions to company profit are the keys to career success. Achieving credibility requires an aggressive, directed effort to complete all tasks on schedule, follow through on all commitments, and offer input based on thorough analysis. Outstanding professional credibility and efforts to help the company achieve prescribed goals are required to get promoted.

13.5 DON'T WORRY ABOUT WHO GETS THE CREDIT

College training and society in general condition us to require recognition for achievement and to want credit for what we've done. It is natural to take pride in accomplishments, and it feels good to share those feelings with others. It is a fatal flaw to apply that philosophy in the workplace by striving to make sure that everyone knows what you have done. Recent college graduates especially must divorce themselves from the conditioned outward need to seek approval and recognition. There is a lot of truth in that trite expression about striving to get your boss promoted so you can be promoted. Don't worry about your boss putting his signature on *your* report. He knows who did the work. Concentrate on getting results and doing a good job, and don't spend time selling your achievements to others. There will be peers and supervisors constantly waiting in the wings to grab credit for your work. Don't worry about it. You can be assured that the recognition will eventually be placed where it rightfully belongs. An employee on the way up doesn't ask for glory or recognition. His satisfaction comes from knowing that he is contributing to the company's profit. Mark Twain once said, "There is no limit to how far a man can go if he doesn't care who gets the credit." Twain was right on!

13.6 ALWAYS EXCEED REQUIREMENTS

Always do a little more than is expected. The effect of that factor on your career cannot be overstated. Develop a frame of mind that says, as a minimum, you will go one extra step in effort for every task. That one extra step is the primary difference between a good employee and an outstanding employee. Following are a few examples of this important concept in action:

A supervisor's phone rings. A good employee answers the phone and offers to take a message; an outstanding employee takes an extra step by asking if he can be of assistance. Don't underestimate the importance of such a small extra step.

An average employee leaves work within two to three minutes after five o'clock; a good employee wraps up loose ends at five o'clock and leaves at ten after the hour. An outstanding employee sometimes leaves at five and sometimes at six, depending on the work load. The outstanding employee is driven by the job, not by the clock.

A supervisor asks that a briefing be prepared on a particular topic. A good employee delivers the briefing as requested. An outstanding employee takes a small extra step by preparing additional material in anticipation of a possible need.

A good employee will ask his supervisor questions that could have been answered elsewhere. An outstanding employee will seek out answers to questions from other sources to avoid bothering the supervisor.

Most employees present problems, questions, and requests for solutions to supervisors. Outstanding employees present the same questions and problems but also offer recommended solutions.

The difference between a highly promotable employee and a run-of-the-mill good employee is measured in contributions and extra effort. If you have the ambition to strive for top management, you should always exceed requirements in virtually every activity in the workplace.

13.7   WORK WELL WITH EVERYONE

Avoid personality conflicts. Working well with all kinds of unique individuals in all levels of management is a prerequisite of promotion. A personality conflict in the initial months of employment can be catastrophic to your career. Forget about whose fault it was, because that is irrelevant. When upper mangement hears of the conflict, the details of who was right or wrong will probably never even be brought up. The supervisors, some of whom may play a key role in your future, will only remember that a personality conflict occurred. One year later, when your name is submitted for promotion, the manager recalls, "Oh year, I remember him, He had a run-in with Joe Mackenzie about a year ago. This new job requires a level-headed person with solid communication and diplomacy skills. We'd better take a pass." You can almost always count on personality conflicts to come back and haunt you. *Caution: Avoid conflicts but always stand your ground on issues of integrity and honesty.*

The importance of working well with people (relational skills) increases proportionately with the level of responsibility of the position. Engineering skills are critical for a project engineer, but when that same engineer is promoted to project manager, the engineering expertise takes a back seat to relational, or people management, skills. *If you are hoping to get promoted, you must exhibit the strengths and personal attributes that are required by positions one and two levels above your current job.* Working well with people is one of those attributes.

I recall a young employee who had a major conflict with his old-timer boss because the boss wanted the young man to use nuts and bolts, not "fancy" folders, to hold together various reports. The demise of this employee's career hinged on this insignificant issue. If you decide to "fall on your sword" over any particular issue, make sure the issue is worth it. Expect to face many annoying idiosyncrasies in your co-workers and supervisors. (I'm sure you'll contribute your share.) Choose your battles carefully; your goal is to win the war, not win a battle about placing reports in "fancy" folders. Avoid personality conflicts. *You must become known as someone who works well with all levels of management—even old-timer supervisors.*

13.8 PAY YOUR DUES

Some of the assignments given to you will require that you muster all of your technical expertise and abilities, while many other tasks will *not* be challenging and may even be demeaning. Dive into each task with the same high level of dedication, enthusiasm, and drive for excellence. Be prepared to pay your dues by welcoming *all* assignments and tasks. Strive to learn and contribute regardless of the perceived importance of the task. An advertising trainee who finds himself immersed in administrative support activities should aggressively learn from the experience, not complain about the lack of direct application of formal training. A young engineer who is expediting parts requisitions should seize the opportunity to learn about vendors and inventory management, not indicate disdain for the assignment. The chemist who is painting and labeling manhole covers should strive to become an expert in the underground chemical disposal network. Don't ever complain about an assignment—just accomplish the task better than anyone while learning as much as possible. Working knee-deep in hydraulic fluid with a college degree sticking out of your back pocket is good for the soul and will serve you well in the future. Jump right in and work your way to the top.

13.9 CONTROLLING YOUR CAREER PATH

You must take an active stance in controlling your own career path. If you simply keep your head down and your nose to the grindstone the only thing that will occur is the removal of your nose. Hardworking employees are appreciated, but not necessarily promoted. Consider the employees in your own work environment. I would bet that you could name employees who have been dedicated and have worked hard for years and yet have *not* been promoted. Perhaps that category includes you!

There are employees in every company who work hard and are fulfilled without moving up the ladder. Such employees form the backbone of industrial America and deserve great respect. Those employees should not be confused, however, with the hard workers who contribute to company success and *want* to be promoted and are waiting for someone to yank them up to a higher-level position. The latter group is often dissatisfied and resentful, because management has never recognized their talent. Working smack dab between the happy hard worker and the ticked-off hard worker, there is an individual who keeps getting promoted time and time again. *The key to promotion is to be active in controlling your career path.* Get your nose off the grindstone and take a look around:

Do your own work first, but look for ways to help co-workers and other departments. I'll draw an example from my own personal experience. I worked in human resources at a facility halfway across the country from the corporate offices. I talked with the corporate human resources staff occasionally, but my primary focus was to serve the local facility. In one discussion I learned that the corporate folks were concerned about turnover. *Without their requesting my assistance*, I completed a study of turnover with maps, charts, and graphs that dramatically depicted problem areas and trends. The study was needed locally, but I also forwarded a copy to the corporate office. The report helped them considerably—and they also learned about an employee out in Podunk who did good work. Shortly thereafter I was moved to the corporate office.

Perhaps a co-worker is having difficulty with an assignment; offer to help, and don't ask for or expect credit. A seed of promotion is planted. Freely share your talent and hard work.

Offer to help your supervisor with his briefing: "I know you're under a tight time frame on this one; is there anything I can do to help?" When he completes the job on schedule, he'll remember that you worked all day on Saturday to help. A seed of promotion is planted. Helping others succeed is a surefire mechanism for getting promoted.

Be socially active in the company. It is not apple-polishing if you join the company's employees association or ski club. Don't just attend the company picnic, chair the entertainment committee. Don't eat in your office if there is a company cafeteria. Sit at different tables every day to gain a broader insight about the company's other departments and let them get to know you. I'm not talking about ingratiating yourself and pouring the salad dressing for upper management; I'm talking about becoming a visible part of the team. When a division head is looking to fill a slot, you'll have a competitive edge if he is familiar with the face that goes with the file.

Develop your own education plan each year. Don't wait for someone to send you to school. Determine your needs and formally request approval to attend. Check with your company's management development department to learn of courses that are available in-house or through such organizations as the American Management Association. Attend night school at a local university. Show that you place a high priority on personal growth and development.

Become active in the community. Contributing to the community is personally fulfilling and will provide valuable management experience.

Get active in professional associations. Become known as a professional in your field. It is not that difficult to write an article for a professional publication and get it published. (Don't write it on company time.) Publications are often searching for material. Being published increases perceived competence and expertise. Show that you are ambitious and creative.

Develop clearly defined career goals. You must have an idea of where you want to go next. Identify positions that you would like to be promoted to and actively prepare for them by taking courses, volunteering for special projects, and learning about the required functions. If ever given the opportunity, subtly mention your excitement about and interest in the position(s) to which you are aspiring. Don't just cross your fingers and dream about getting promoted; do something about it.

Conclusion

There is a lot of hard work involved in the career-controlling actions discussed in this chapter. It is much easier to keep your nose to the grindstone and hope that someone will promote you, but don't count on that happening.

Most employees are not willing to expend the tremendous effort necessary to climb the corporate ladder, and instead will rely on the annual performance appraisal to get them promoted. Those employees will typically receive small merit raises and possibly a small promotion or two spread over many years—and that's OK. Those employees are the heartbeat of the corporation. If you are extremely ambitious and have established high aspirations, you'll need to take direct control of your career. The avenues of action presented in this chapter will form the foundation. It's easy to talk about extra effort, but it is much harder to follow through consistently. Employment can be an exciting and enjoyable part of your life—if you are in control of your destiny. My warmest regards are extended to you with the hope that you achieve the happiness and fulfillment that you seek. Good luck.

Recommended Reading

There are hundreds of books on the job search and career counseling. I highly recommend the following two books.

Resume Help   Lathrop, Richard. *Who's Hiring Who.*   Berkeley, California : Ten Speed Press, 1977.

Lathrop's book is a tremendous resource for resume-writing support. His insight and examples are worth the investment of your time.

Counseling Help   Bolles, Richard N.   *What Color Is Your Parachute?*   Berkeley, California: Ten Speed Press, 1986.

Bolles' book is organized about as well as my family-room closet, but there is some good counseling in it if you look hard enough. Chapter Five, "What Do You Want to Do," and Chapter Six, "Where Do You Want to Do It" are good counseling aids. If you don't have access to a placement or professional job counselor, Bolles can help you figure out what you might like to do.

JOB HUNTING CALENDAR*

"Open Season Year Round"

JANUARY
- Year end bus. closing
- Minimal hiring
- Holiday recuperation

FEBRUARY
- College visits back on
- Moderate hiring activity
- New positions approved
- Business projections complete

MARCH
- Heavy college recruiting
- Peak hiring activity
- Summer jobs proposed

APRIL
- Heavy college recruiting
- Summer jobs approved
- Peak hiring activity

MAY
- Reduced college recruiting
- Peak activity for job changers
- Heavy middle mgmt. hires
- Peak hiring activity

JUNE
- Minimal college recruiting
- College grads enter real world
- Middle mgmt. hires

JULY

- Low hiring activity
- Decision makers on vacation
- Manpower planning for fall recruitment

AUGUST

- Decision makers still on vacation
- Moderate hiring activity
- Strategic planning for following year begins

SEPTEMBER

- Manpower plan approved
- College recruiting begins
- Heavy hiring activity

OCTOBER

- Heavy college recruiting
- Moderate hiring activity
- Turnover percentage goes down

NOVEMBER

- Heavy college recruiting
- Moderate hiring activity
- Turnover drops

DECEMBER

- Minimal turnover
- Minimal recruiting
- Good month for information interviews

*Industries tied to seasons or other cyclical factors have unique hiring calendars.

INDEX